F3D Skyknight

In Action®

Written by Alan C. Carey

Squadron/Signal Publications

Cover Art by Don Greer

Line Illustrations by Melinda Turnage

(Front Cover) Major Elswin Dunn and his radar operator MSgt. Lawrence J. Fortrin of VMF(N)-513 in their Douglas F3D-2 Skyknight, WF/8 BuNo 124615, score a night kill against a Chinese MiG-15 over North Korea during the evening of 12 January 1953. The MiG was the fourth of six enemy aircraft destroyed in the air by the squadron's Skyknights between November 1952 and January 1953.

(Back Cover) F3D-2 ATG/404, BuNo 127939, from the Tophatters of VF-14 leaves the USS *Intrepid* (CVA-11) during carrier qualifications with the Skyknight on 13 October 1954.

About the In Action® Series

In Action® books, despite the title of the genre, are books that trace the development of a single type of aircraft, armored vehicle, or ship from prototype to the final production variant. Experimental or "one-off" variants can also be included. Our first *In Action®* book was printed in 1971.

Hardcover ISBN 978-0-89747-686-7
Softcover ISBN 978-0-89747-685-0
Proudly printed in the U.S.A.
Copyright 2012 Squadron/Signal Publications
1115 Crowley Drive, Carrollton, TX 75006-1312 U.S.A.

Military/Combat Photographs and Snapshots

If you have any photos of aircraft, armor, soldiers, or ships of any nation, particularly wartime snapshots, why not share them with us and help make Squadron/Signal's books all the more interesting and complete in the future? Any photograph sent to us will be copied and returned. Electronic images are preferred. The donor will be fully credited for any photos used. Please send them to:

Squadron/Signal Publications
1115 Crowley Drive
Carrollton, TX 75006-1312 U.S.A.
www.SquadronSignalPublications.com

(Title Page) EF-10B Skyknight RM/3 BuNo 124619, shown here in February 1969, was a former VMCJ-2 EF-10 before VMCJ-1 acquired this aircraft and operated it from Đà Nẵng, South Vietnam. The *Snoopy* logo on the tail was the unofficial mascot of VMCJ-1. (Terry Panopalis Collection via Tommy H. Thomason)

Acknowledgments

I truly appreciate Paul Bless for providing technical data on the Douglas F3D Skyknight along with Wayne "Flash" Whitten of the Marine Corps Aviation Reconnaissance Association and Robert Dorr who provided information on the aircraft's role during the Vietnam War. Gary Verver, the creator of the website: A Photographic History of NAF & VX-5 at NOTS China Lake provided additional technical assistance on the aircraft's role in air-to-air missile testing. Mark Aldrich came through with a considerable number of images while Richard Dann made my life easier by furnishing the line art for this book. Thanks are also due to Tommy H. Thomason and Paul Bless for providing and clarifying technical data for the F3D series. (Photo credits are included with the captions)

Introduction

The introduction of Germany's Messerschmitt Me 262 jet fighter over the skies of Western Europe in the summer of 1944 revolutionized aerial warfare and ushered in a new era of military aviation. Before the end of World War II, the British introduced the Gloster Meteor Mk I, while the Lockheed P-80A Shooting Star became the U.S. Army Air Force's first operational jet fighter. The U.S. Navy unofficially entered the jet age when it acquired two Bell YP-59A Airacomets in December 1943 and three P-80As in 1945 for familiarization and carrier suitability trials.

The Navy officially entered the jet-age when it awarded McDonnell Aircraft Company a production contract for an FD-1 fighter in March 1945. Delivery of this aircraft, later designated as the FH-1 Phantom, to naval squadrons began in July 1947. For nocturnal work during the post-war years, the Air Force relied on the Northrop P-61 Black Widow and the North American F-82F/G Twin Mustang, while the Navy utilized the Vought F4U-5N Corsair during the late-1940s, and the Marine Corps operated the Corsair and the Grumman F7F-3N Tigercat. Both the Air Force and the Navy seriously began research for a jet-powered night fighter immediately after the war. The Army Air Force requested such a design in late 1945 and awarded Northrop a contract to build the Northrop F-89 Scorpion. Meanwhile, the U.S. Navy issued a request to leading American aircraft manufacturers for a two-seat jet aircraft with long-range radar and excellent performance at high altitudes. Specifically, the Bureau of Aeronautics issued a requirement for a carrier-based jet night fighter with a top speed in excess of 500 m.p.h. at 40,000 feet, and with an airborne radar system able to detect enemy aircraft at a distance of 125 miles.

When Douglas began preliminary design studies for a jet-powered night fighter, the technology simply did not exist to reduce the size and weight of airborne radar systems. This was still the era of vacuum tubes; the transistor, which would reduce the weight and space of avionic systems, would not make its appearance until the mid-1950s. The solution was to design a jet fighter with an unconventional airframe around a radar system with the ability to track targets 125 miles away. Such an electronics package would require a housing large enough for a large radar dish and associated equipment. Douglas picked veteran aeronautical engineer Ed Heinemann to head the design study team at the company's facility in El Segundo, California. A daunting task faced Heinemann and his team as they began preliminary design work in October 1945. This would be the first jet strictly designed as an all-weather fighter from the ground up and, if successful, it would be the Navy's first Douglas-built jet fighter. But the Navy's requirements for the aircraft seemed impossible to meet according to Heinemann.

"The original specification for this aircraft came as somewhat of a shock to the designers. High speed requirements appeared to be completely incompatible with the requirements of a two-place cockpit arrangement and a large space forward of the cockpit required for electronic night flying equipment. It was only after trying many arrangements of equipment, crew, fuel, and power plants that the final arrangement of the F3D was chosen."

Ed Heinemann realized that meeting the Navy's speed, altitude, and range requirements

An F4U-5N Corsair of VMF(N)-114 in all her splendor, sports overall glossy sea blue, and white number and letter codes as she cruises somewhere over the Atlantic, possibly near the Florida Keys or Bahama Islands. The U.S. Navy relied on the F4U-5N as its carrier-based night fighter from the late 1940s and throughout the Korean War, while the Marine Corps utilized both the F4U-5N and F7F-3N Tigercat as its shore-based night fighters. (John E. Adamic via Mark Adamic)

The Navy envisioned the Grumman F7F Tigercat as the service's post-World War II carrier-based night fighter but structural problems and poor handling characteristics during carrier trials relegated the aircraft to operations with land-based Marine units. The F7F-3N variant saw service in the Korean conflict with VMF(N)-513 and 542. Both squadrons would later transition to the F3D Skyknight. (Tommy H. Thomason)

for the F3D required a conscious effort to reduce the aircraft's weight and to design exterior features that would limit drag. When Douglas first conceived the Skyknight in 1945, calculations showed that the minimum combat radius requirements could barely be met. To do so required a non-conventional windshield for a jet fighter and internal housing of radar antennas. After testing various arrangements, Douglas selected a large, flat, bullet-resistant windshield because it offered the lowest possible drag and aided in gun-sighting and night vision. To reduce drag and weight according to Heinemann, "It was aerodynamically essential that all radar antennas to be mounted within the aircraft's normal contours. This required a considerable amount of antenna research and the development of non-metallic (fiberglass) structures such as the fuselage nose cone, tail components, vertical tail cap, and dorsal fin, to house various forms of antenna."

Heinemann's team doggedly worked on the design and by the end of March 1946, their mockup was ready for the Navy's inspection. Competing against Douglas were Grumman, Curtiss, and Kaiser-Fleetwings Company, with the principal competitor being Grumman's four-engine XF9F-1. The Navy awarded Douglas a letter of intent on 3 April 1946 for delivery of three prototypes and a static test article, but the Navy hedged its bet on Douglas in case its design ran into trouble, by awarding a second letter of intent to Grumman for two XF9F-1 prototypes. Douglas became the sole heir of the project when Grumman dropped out the competition after determining that the engineering and operating problems of developing its four-engine aircraft made the project unfeasible. Therefore, Grumman transferred developmental funds for the study of a jet-powered carrier-based single-engine day fighter that would eventually become the Navy's famed F9F-2 Panther.

The Curtis XF-87 Blackhawk was another night fighter design competing for a military contract. It lost out, however, primarily due to underpowered engines. It surpassed the length of the F3D by nearly 17 feet. (Rich Dann)

A test probe on its wing tip, the first XF3D-1 Skyknight prototype BuNo 121457 soars over California. It first took to the air in March 1948. The prototypes J34-WE-22 axial-flow turbojet engines did not provide adequate thrust and Douglas fitted subsequent production models with the J34-WE-34. (San Diego Aerospace Museum, SDAM)

The U.S. Air Force's answer for a new all-weather night fighter to replace the P-61 Black Widow was the Northrop F-89 Scorpion. (Rich Dann)

XF3D

Heinemann's team came up with a design for the F3D that featured a mid-wing configuration that made the aircraft less aerodynamically and esthetically pleasing than other sleek jet interceptors of the period. But considerable thought had been put into designing an aircraft that could house all the necessary avionics, armament, and a two-man crew. The Skyknight's fuselage was stubby, squat, and wide at the front with a bulbous cockpit while the rear portion tapered into a more conventional shape. The designers chose a hydraulically operated tricycle landing gear configuration for increased stability and safety during high-speed takeoffs and landings. The main landing gear retracted into the inner wing panels while the nose wheel retracted rearward. The aircraft's relatively low ground clearance required the installation of a small auxiliary tail wheel to the tailskid in front of the arresting hook to protect the tail structure during takeoffs and landings. The Skyknight also incorporated speed brakes that deployed outward from the aft part of the fuselage to decelerate the aircraft for carrier landing approaches or to keep it from exceeding its maximum speed limits while in a dive.

Armament for the XF3D-1 through the production versions consisted of four 20mm cannons mounted under the nose, with 200 rounds-per gun. Maximum external stores for the aircraft included the capability to carry a maximum 4,000 pounds of bombs and rockets mounted on inboard wing racks. The electronics package for production models would be equipped with the most sophisticated airborne radar of the period – the Westinghouse AN/APQ-35 radar armament control system. The first two XF3Ds, which were to be used for development flight tests by Douglas and structural demonstration and carrier suitability tests by the Navy, were not equipped with the radar system. Contrary to suggestions by some sources, there is no evidence that the World War II-era SCR-720 radar was ever installed in any F3D. It is possible that Douglas and/or the Navy considered it for an interim capability due to development problems with the AN/APQ-35.

The prototypes used two Westinghouse 11-stage J34-WE-22 axial-flow turbojet engines with 3,000 pounds of thrust each, burning JP-3 fuel or 115/145 AVGAS, and housed in nacelles below the wings on each side of the fuselage. The engines were easily accessible and changing them only required removing the cowling and dropping the engine onto a handling truck with a standard bomb hoist. This configuration made it possible to complete an engine change in approximately one hour. The F3D's night mission, which required it to remain on station for extended periods, required the aircraft to have a larger fuel capacity than a typical jet fighter. The fuel for the XF3D was located internally in

The first prototype XF3D-1, seen here in 1949, features relatively small engine nacelles and an early skid-type bumper. The white stripes identified the steps for climbing into the cockpit. (SDAM via Mark Aldrich)

fuel cells within the fuselage above the engines and aft of the pilot's compartment. The cells' capacity was 1,290 gallons. Production units could carry external fuel stores in 150-gallon drop tanks underneath each wing near the folding joint. Heinemann's team thought of installing wing tip tanks like that of the F-80. "Considerable thought was given to the installation of wing tip tanks. They were decided against, however, owing to the serious problem of obtaining the necessary lateral control with one tank empty, the increase in wing weight resulting from landing loads with tanks full, and the problem of filling tanks when wings are folded," Heinemann said.

The size, shape, and seating arrangement of the Skyknight's side-by-side cockpit configuration resembled that of a transport more than a typical fighter. Pilots, radar operators, ground crews, and others would refer it as "Willy the Whale" due to its unconventional shape, which did bear some resemblance to the sea mammal. Entry to the cockpit required climbing up the engine nacelle onto the wing, and walking forward across the cockpit's roof to a square glass hatch. After sliding the hatch to the rear, the pilot and RO dropped down into their seats.

The pressurized cabin featured an instrument panel and console designed for night work. The lighting system prevented glare in the pilot's eyes and assured constant lighting of all gauges and dials. Lettering and numbers were etched in transparent Lucite and red lights illuminated the entire panel from behind. That way, a failure of a bulb did not disrupt instrument visibility, as remaining lights would continue to illuminate the panel and console. Rearview mirrors located in front of the pilot and RO helped with rearward visibility, which was restricted by the cockpit's rear bulkhead. Other cockpit features included an air conditioning and heating system, cigarette lighter, ashtray, and even a thermos jug.

The F3D's most unusual feature was its revolutionary crew escape system that was unlike that of any other aircraft at the time. The Skyknight's side-by-side seat configuration posed a major engineering problem when it came to the point where a crew had to bail out of the aircraft. Medical studies conducted at the time revealed the impossibility of bailing out of the aircraft without serious injury to the crew since it would have been highly probable that an occupant would hit the high tail surfaces or elevators during a normal egress. Douglas considered ejection seats but the additional weight, reconfiguring the seating arrangement, and requiring a sliding cockpit that would compromise pressurization, ultimately ruled out such a design. Company engineers studied other methods of egress before settling on an escape chute located under and aft of the cockpit.

To activate the escape system a crewmember pulled an escape chute door emergency release handle located on the central console. This would blow off the rear half of the chute

Three-quarter view of the first prototype shows the main armament of the F3D consisting of four 20mm cannons. This aircraft, along with BuNos 121458 and 121459, was one of three XF3D-1 prototypes and were noticeably different from later, production models due to the smaller housing for the -22 engines. (Clay Jansson via Tailhook)

exit hatch in the belly between the engines, while the front half would extend serving as a windbreak. After pulling the upper escape hatch release handle, each crewmember would then pivot around in his seat, grab a vaulting bar behind the seat, kick open the upper escape door, and slide down the chute feet-first, one crewmember at a time. Although escaping head first was not totally ruled out, it was highly discouraged.

After 11 months of fine-tuning the XF3D-1, the first prototype, BuNo 121457, took to the air. Russell W. Thaw, a test pilot with 24 years' experience, took off from Muroc Dry Lake, California, on 23 March 1948 and gave the aircraft its first test flight. The second prototype first flew on 6 June, followed by the third on 7 October. Douglas test pilots conducted flight tests involving spin recovery, single-engine performance, escape chute reliability, radar interception, and carrier suitability.

One problem noted during early speed trials with the XF3D-1 pertained to stability and control. During early speed tests, Thaw felt a mildly high-frequency vibration in the forward part of the fuselage. Using an oscillograph, engineers recorded the frequency of the vibration and were able to trace the flutter to the elevator trim tab. Minor modifications corrected the trouble.

Evaluation continued at Muroc Dry Lake, where in October 1948 the Air Force became interested in the Skyknight for a time as an interim replacement for the Northrop F-89 Scorpion all-weather interceptor, which was suffering from development problems. The USAF decided to acquire the Lockheed F-94 Starfire until Northrop could correct the Scorpion's deficiencies.

Russell Thaw flew a number of flights to test the XF3D-1's unique escape system with the Navy's Parachute Experimental Unit which conducted 22 successful bail-out flights over the Salton Sea at El Centro, California, at speeds ranging from 139 to 444 m.p.h. Performance figures for the XF3D-1 were – speed 518 m.p.h. at sea level and 525 m.p.h. at 20,000 feet; service ceiling was 33,000 feet and range was 1,126 miles with internal and wing tank fuel stores. Initial rate of climb was 3,710 feet per minute.

Decked out in glossy sea blue, the first prototype soars over Southern California. A hatch located above the cockpit allowed for entry into the cabin. (Author's Collection)

Douglas designers chose a hydraulically operated tricycle landing gear configuration for increased stability and safety during high-speed takeoffs and landings. (SDAM via Mark Aldrich)

The first two prototypes were not equipped with a radar system. The third prototype, however, was equipped with the AN/APQ-35 for evaluation. (Tailhook via Clay Jannson)

Admiral Forrest P. Sherman, Chief of Naval Operations, climbs aboard the second prototype for a familiarization flight with Lt. C.B. Smith as pilot at NAS Patuxent River in late 1949. (Author's Collection)

This rear view of the second prototype highlights the aircraft's natural metal exhausts. The cant of the exhausts created problems during carrier operations as they had the tendency to burn a carrier's wooden flight deck. (SDAM via Mark Aldrich)

The last three digits of the bureau number are clearly visible on the first prototype as it flies over Edwards AFB, California. A trio of Boeing B-29s are parked at a hangar in the background. (SDAM via Mark Aldrich)

In about 1949, the second prototype now carries the markings of Naval Air Test Center (NATC) at NAS Patuxent River, where the aircraft is undergoing carrier evaluation testing. (Author's Collection)

A member of Navy Parachute Facility El Centro, California, slids from the unique "Laundry Chute" of the XF3D-1 from an altitude of 5,000 feet during testing of the aircraft's escape system. (Author's Collection)

This sequence of images taken in December 1949 shows one of 22 successful jumps completed by the Navy Parachute Facility during testing of the Skyknight's escape system. (Author Collection)

XF3D-1 BuNo 121457 rests on the tarmac at NAS Patuxent River, Maryland, where its updated control systems are being tested in June 1949. Since the Skyknight was designed for shipboard operations, the wings folded for storage. Built at Douglas' El Segundo plant in California, it was first flown by Russell W. Thaw from Muroc Dry Lake (later Edwards AFB) in March 1948. Douglas and the Navy continued to use this and the other two prototypes for flight testing and evaluation of the radar and escape systems. Overall color is glossy sea blue with white codes and light gray wheels. The Skyknight showed promise at first but structural problems, design flaws, and insufficient power restricted the aircraft's use aboard carriers. Production aircraft for both the F3D-1 and -2 were sent primarily to units tasked with land-based operations. The Skyknight's shortcomings would normally have limited its service life, but with its large, rugged airframe, the aircraft could house a wide array of electronic packages, and so it managed to remain in the Navy's inventory until 1970. (Clay Jansson via Rich Dann)

Development

XF3D-1 Early

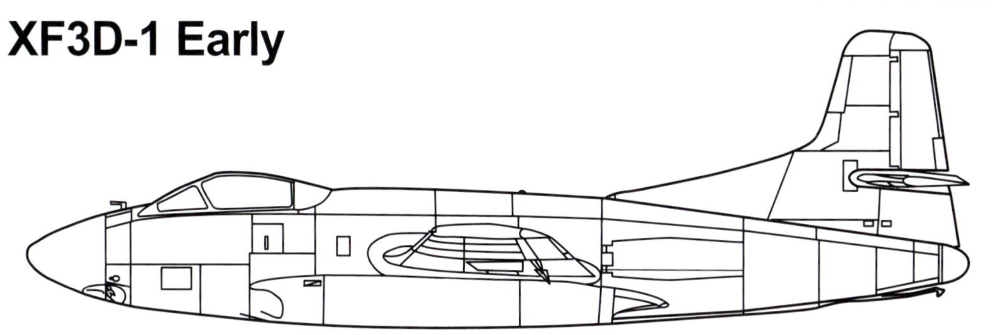

XF3D-1 Late

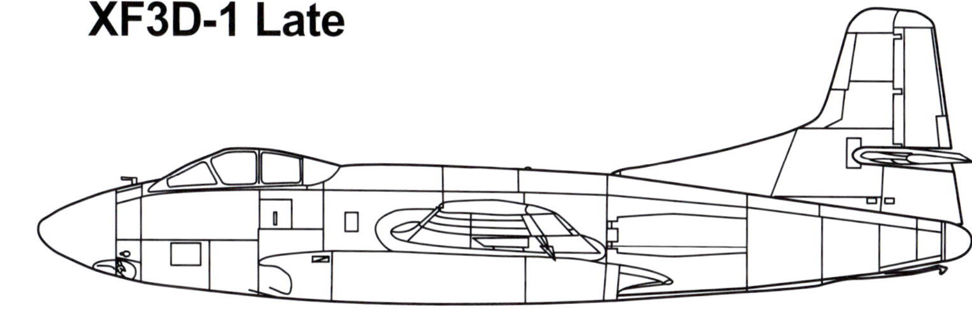

F3D-1

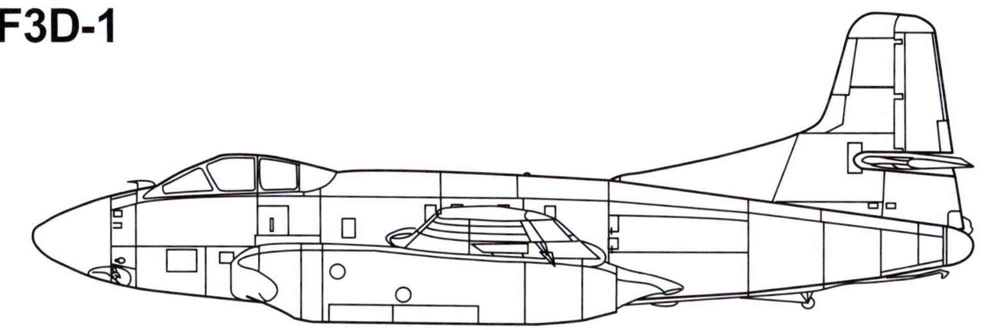

F3D-1M

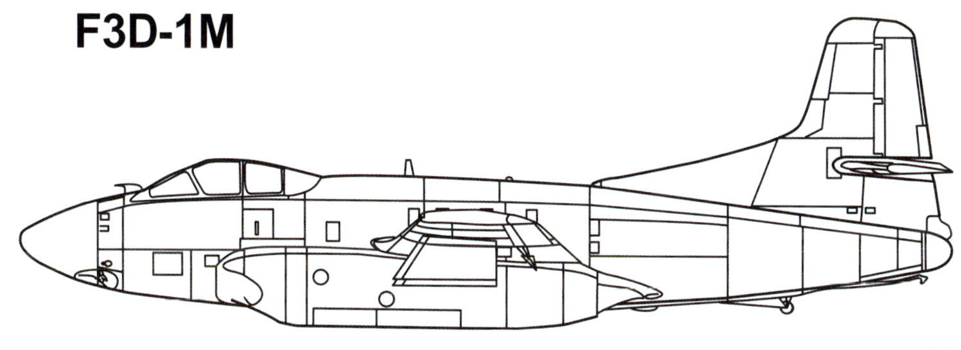

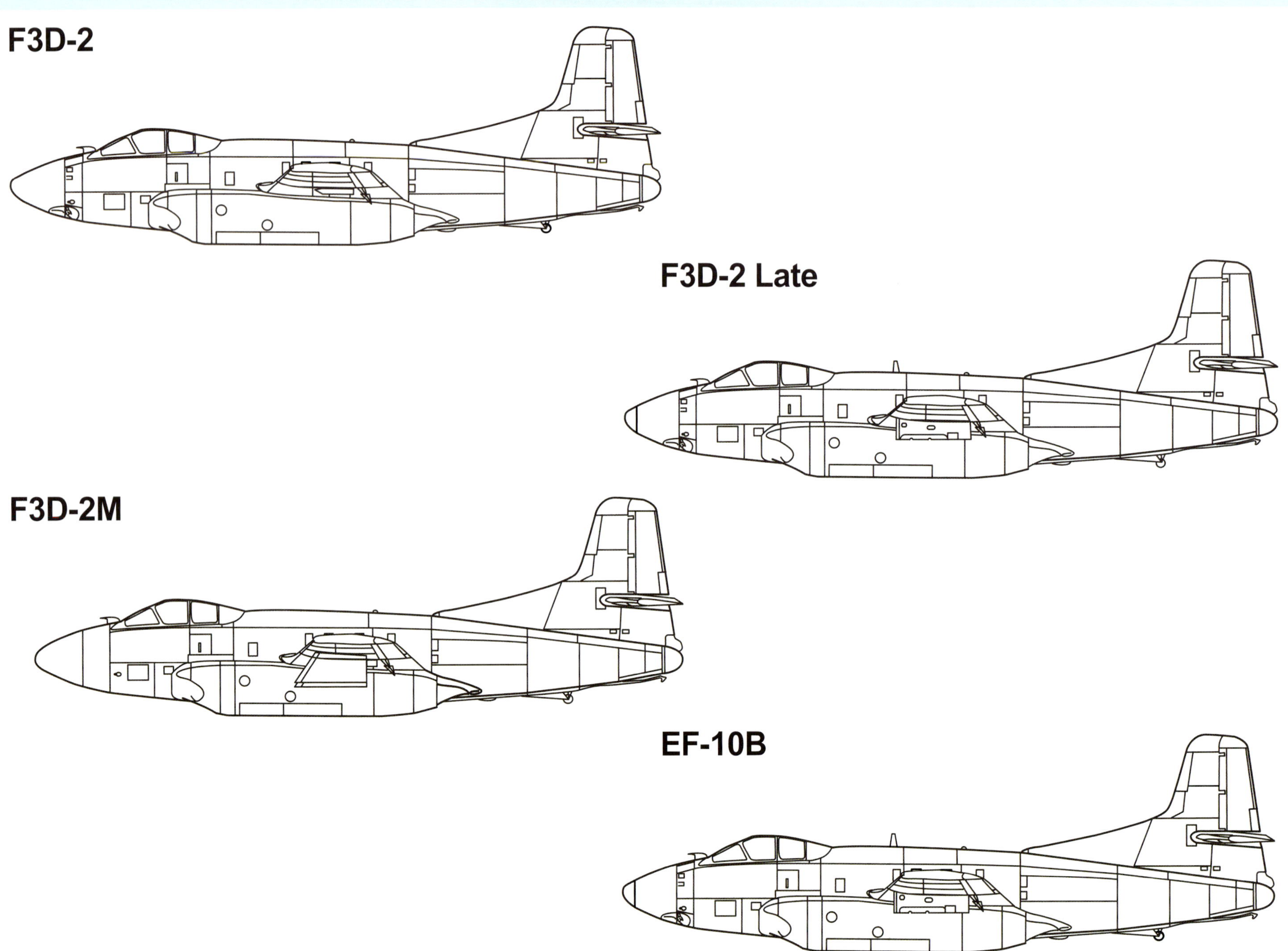

F3D-2
F3D-2 Late
F3D-2M
EF-10B

F3D-1

Disappointed with Grumman's F7F Tigercat, the Navy wanted its replacement to serve as a carrier-based all-weather fighter, and began carrier suitability trials of the F3D. Navy tests on XF3D-1 BuNo 121458 at NATC Patuxent River between 4 October 1949 and 1 February 1950, revealed a number of deficiencies that delayed the acceptance of the Skyknight as either a day or night carrier-borne fighter.

One of the primary problems was the aircraft's incompatibility with the carrier arresting gear in use at the time. Problems ranged from excessive time to spot and tension the aircraft on the catapult to difficulty in attaching the catapult bridle and holdback assembly due to the close proximity of the engine air intakes and exhaust. The heat from the exhaust also had the tendency to burn the carrier's wooden decks. Additional structural faults included a tendency for the tail hook to bend on landing, as the tail bumper was too short and too weak to withstand carrier landings. A larger tail bumper, new handling techniques, and a different catapult-launching bridle helped alleviate some of the problems during subsequent trials with the F3D-1 and F3D-2.

In flight tests the prototype's J34-WE-22 engines failed to deliver the desired thrust. To improve performance, Douglas proposed installing twin Westinghouse J46 turbojets, each with 4,600 pounds of thrust. The company also hoped to promote the aircraft to the Air Force by offering the F3D-1 with either the J-34-15 or J-34-17 afterburning engines. Either way, the Skyknight required larger nacelles to accommodate the Dash-15 and 17. In the end, the Air Force chose the F-89 Scorpion over the Skyknight. Development issues with the J-46 forced Douglas to go with the J-34-38, but then the -38 experienced problems too, and ultimately the company opted to install the J34-WE-34s, each rated at 3,250 pounds of thrust, on production aircraft. Until the 34-WE-34 became available, however, early F3D-1s retained the J34-WE-22 power plant as the XF3D. Performance figures for the F3D-1 were: maximum speed – 530 m.p.h. at sea level, 565 m.p.h. at 20,000 feet, 425 m.p.h. at 40,000 feet; service 34,000 feet and range 1,318 miles with internal and wing tank fuel stores. Initial rate of climb was 1,960 feet per minute.

The F3D-1's airframe was similar to that of the XF3D-1, but was fitted with a stronger tail bumper wheel. The F3D-1 main gear doors also remained open while those of the prototypes retracted when the gear was fully extended. The F3D-1 also initially featured an additional speed brake located on the fuselage's belly in the configuration of the company's Skyraider. The bottom speed brake was added to the F3D-1 because the aft fuselage speed brakes had been reduced in size due to the aircraft's larger nacelles (designed to accommodate the projected use of the J-34 to 46 series engines). Testing at NAS Patuxent River, however showed that the extended lower speed brake was prone to damage from ejected links and shell casings when the 20mm cannons were fired. As consequence, the lower speed brake was deactivated and, later, eliminated altogether. Two series of F3D-1s were built: Series A (10) had the lower speed brake; Series B (18) was built without the lower brake.

The Skyknight's Westinghouse AN/APQ-35, housed in the nose of the aircraft, actually consisted of three separate radars with four different radar scopes: the AN/APS-

The two images on this page illustrate how the engine nacelles of the prototype and production F3D-1 differed in size. This Douglas XF3D-1 Skyknight BuNo 121458 is equipped with the original nacelles that housed 3,000-pound thrust Westinghouse J34-WE-22c engines. (Clay Jansson via Tailhook Association)

The first production F3D-1, BuNo 123741, displays the larger engine nacelles intended to accommodate more powerful engines such as the J34-We-38 and J46-WE-3 turbo jets. (SDAM via Mark Aldrich)

The early tail-skid and hook configuration, shown here on the first prototype, proved troublesome during carrier suitability trails during late 1949 and early 1950 and the Navy recommended modifications.

The heavier tailhook and larger tail-skid, shown here on BuNo 123745, were installed on production F3D-1 and -2s as a result of recommendations coming from earlier carrier testing with the prototypes.

21, airborne long-range search and intercept radar; AN/APG-26 airborne gun aim radar; and AN/APS-28, airborne tail warning radar; the latter being installed on the F3D-2. Maximum effective range of the over-450-pound system depended on the size of the target and factors like altitude and weather conditions. The AN/APS-21 search radar – with its 170-degree forward, up, and down sweep – located and tracked a target's altitude and position. Effective range depended on the size of the target, larger targets having greater range. This system, located in the radar operator's position, worked jointly with the AN/APS-26 firing control system. When a target entered close range, the AN/APS-21 handed tracking over to the AN/APS-26 and then went back to scanning for new targets. The targeting radar could provide the pilot with a firing solution in less than a second. Additional communication and navigational equipment included the AN/ARC-27 VHF radio, AN/APN-1 radio altimeter, AN/APX-6 IFF equipment, and the AN/ARA-25 direction finder group.

The four separate radars making up the APQ-35 made the system too complex for a pilot to operate on his own. A highly skilled radar operator was needed and even for him, it was a difficult system to use. The radar panel in front of the RO featured a variety of knobs, switches, and three radarscopes that would frighten a novice and just starting and calibrating the system required a five-step procedure. First, the RO had to be satisfied that at least one of the aircraft's engines was running near full power to provide adequate electricity to the radar. Second, once the APS-21 was receiving enough power, he turned on the invertors that produced high-voltage alternating currents. Once the radar received enough "juice," the RO turned on and calibrated the tail warning set and then the gun-laying system. Operating the AN/APQ-35 required considerable finesse on the part of the RO plus coordination with the pilot. Moving the elevation of the radar dish up or down required the use of a toggle switch and it was difficult to get the elevation centered. Another problem was that the dish had a tendency to swing from side-to-side as the aircraft banked which required close communication between the pilot and RO so that the latter could anticipate turns and adjust the dish's elevation to keep track of a target.

Unfortunately for the manufacturer and the Navy, the new engines provided little increase in thrust. Production was limited to only 28 of the F3D-1s (BuNos 123741 to 123768), which the Navy and Marine Corps used as training aircraft until the expected delivery of the updated F3D-2 with the J-46 engines. The first production F3D-1 flew on 13 February 1950 and the Navy took delivery in August that year. The first Skyknight series entered operational service with the Navy Composite Squadron (VC-3) at Moffett Field, California, in December 1950. Soon afterward, VMF(N)-542, at El Toro MCAS, received F3D-1s and began training with them for eventual deployment to Korea. Along with those received by VC-3 and VMF(N)-542, the remaining F3D-1s remained stateside for further developmental testing with NATC at Patuxent, Air Development Squadron Four (VX-4), Point Mugu and Naval Ordnance Test Station (NOTS) China Lake. The Skyknight was the first Navy jet equipped with air-to-air missiles. VX-4, Point Mugu and China Lake flew a number of F3D-1s with a modified hardpoint under each wing to test a variety of missile systems. Those F3D-1s that were still in service in September 1962 were redesignated as F-10A aircraft, pursuant to a new Tri-service designation system.

Lt. R.C. Timm is at the controls of this early F3D-1 seen in this color-enhanced image from September 1950. The 28 F3D-1s produced were sent to units for further development testing, missile testing, and for training pilots and radar operators for transition to the F3D-2. (National Archives)

The wing hard points visible on this early F3D-1 in September 1950 are for mounting external fuel tanks or bombs. (National Archives)

Pilot Lt. R.C. Timm has extended the speed brakes on his early F3D-1 at NATC Patuxent River on 5 September 1950. (National Archives)

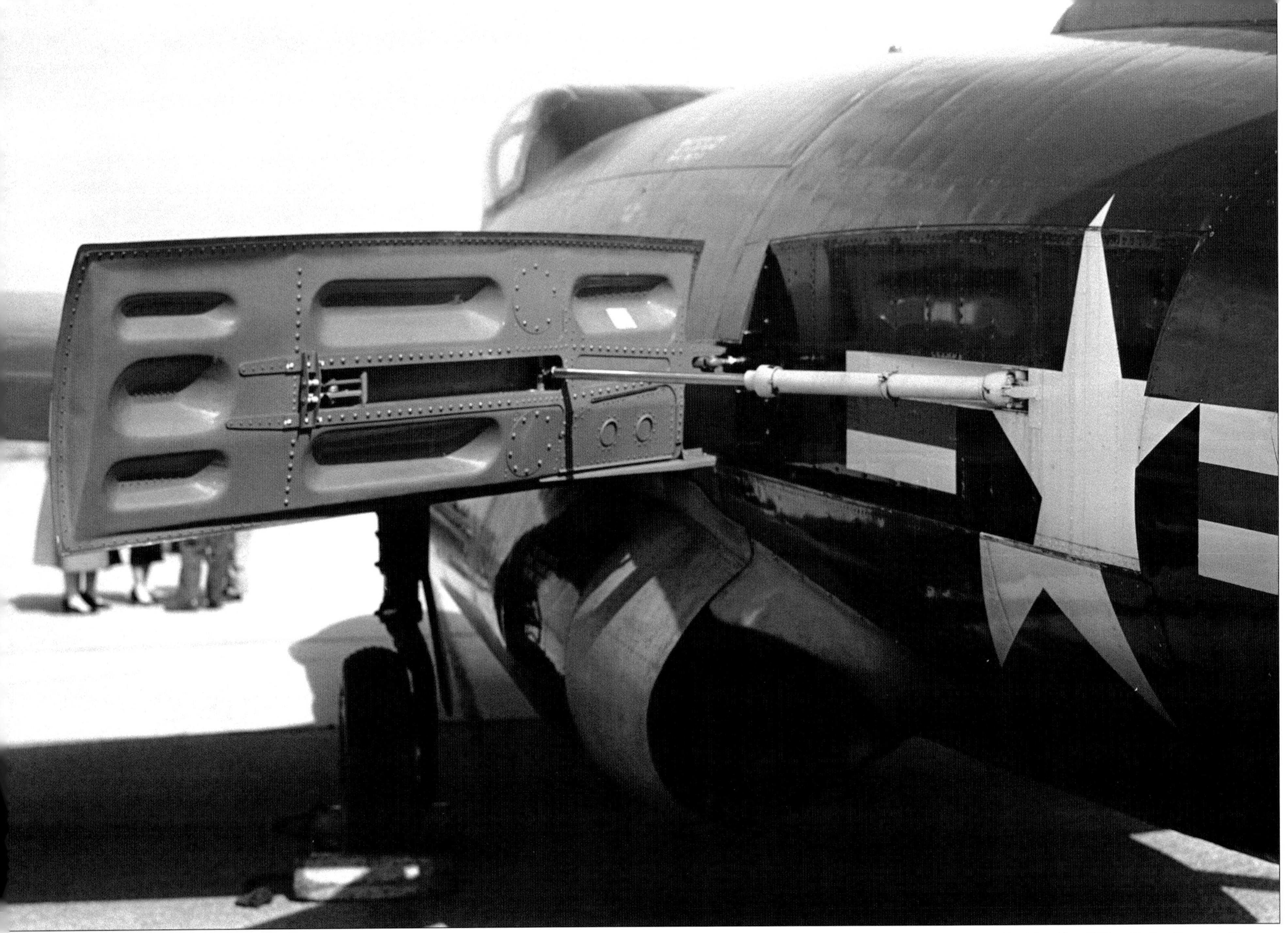

This photograph taken by Pete Bulban shows the hydraulically actuated speed brake on an F3D-2 with the star and bars painted on the inside. (Jay Miller Collection via Tommy H. Thomason)

NATC tactical test aircraft (TT-13) F3D-1, BuNo 123743, sits on the tarmac at NAS Pax River in about 1952. This third production unit of the series took part in early carrier suitability testing before being modified as a missile-armed F3D-1M, operating from China Lake and Point Mugu. (Clay Jansson via Tailhook Association)

NATC received BuNo 123744 in the fall of 1950 and operated it until 1956, when it was transferred to China Lake for more testing. It wound up in 1959 at NAF Litchfield Park, Arizona, where it was finally scrapped along with her sisters. (SDAM via Mark Aldrich)

NATC BuNo 123743, seen here from starboard, sports the typical over all glossy sea blue with white numbers, stenciling, and service marking on lower wing surface, with light gray main wheels, and candy-striped tailhook. (Author Collection)

F3D-1, BuNo 123745, at NAS Pax River, was acquired by NATC and used for the first Automatic Carrier Landing System Test (ALCS) conducted at Niagara Falls Airport, New York, during May 1954. The ALCS system was developed by Bell and designated as the AN/SPN-10. (SDAM via Mark Aldrich)

The speed brakes are deployed on this early F3D-1, possibly BuNo 123748. The bottom dive brake was prone to damage from expended shell casings from the nose cannons and was eliminated on the F3D-2. (Author's Collection)

Lacking identifying unit codes, BuNo 123747 was later converted to an F3D-1M to test missile systems at Naval Missile Test Center Point Mugu, California, and remained in that capacity well into the 1950s. (SDAM via Mark Aldrich)

Cruising above California, BuNo 123748 sports its name and that of its manufacturer in a promotion of Douglas Aircraft's first military jet. The aircraft was also modified to the F3D-1M configuration. (SDAM via Mark Aldrich)

Another F3D-1 converted to an F3D-1M was No. 751 (BuNo 123751) shown here with red intake lips and light gray nose wheel at NAS Patxuent. The FT designation on the nose stands for Flight Test. (Clay Jansson via Tailhook Association)

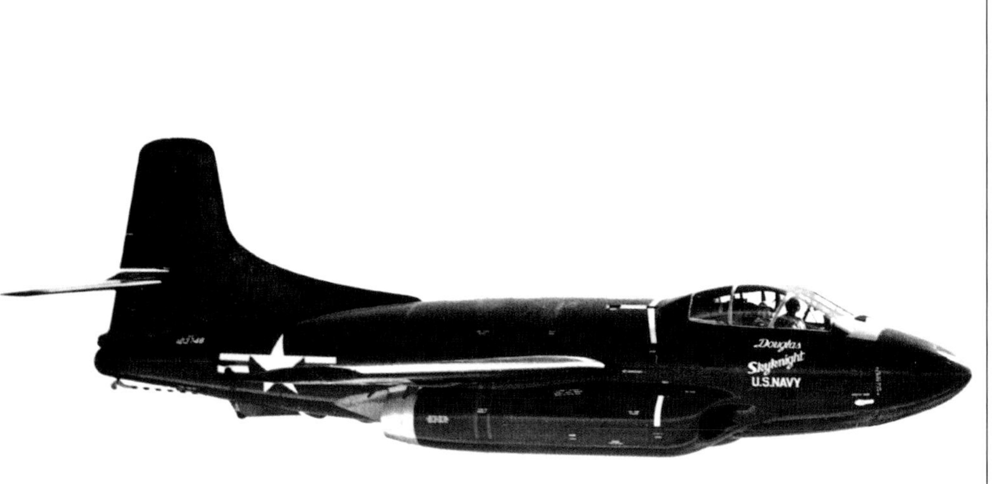

Some signs of wear are visible on the nose of No. 751 at the NATC's tactical test division. The aircraft's nose was unusually wide in order to house the Westinghouse APQ-35 radar system. (Author's Collection)

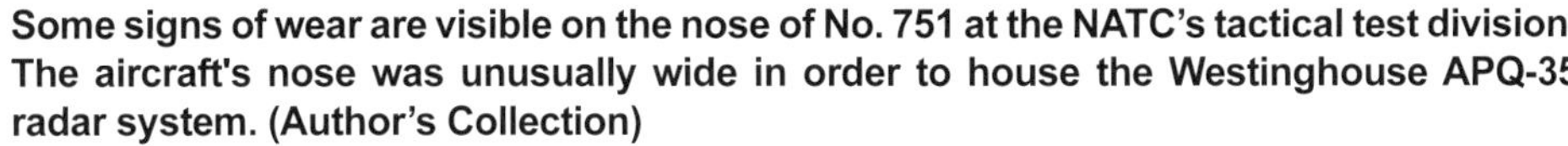

Factory fresh from the El Segundo plant and lacking identifying unit markings, this glossy blue F3D-1, BuNo 123762, is ready for an air show at Los Angeles Airport (LAX) during October 1951. (Mark Aldrich)

Parked on the tarmac at Armitage Field at China Lake during 1951, BuNo 123755 went on to serve as a test vehicle at NAS Quonset Point, Rhode Island, and Patuxent River. (U.S. Navy via Gary Verver)

BuNo 123754 is in the foreground of this group of F3D-1s of Navy Composite Squadron Three (VC-3) on the tarmac at NAS Moffet Field, California, in June 1951. (Jim Berry Collection via Tailhook Association)

VC-3 became the first Navy unit to receive production F3D-1s for training pilots and ROs. NP/76, 75, and 77 are shown over San Francisco on 12 March 1951. (Jim Berry Collection via Tailhook Association)

The VC-3 NP/75, BuNo 123763, flying over San Francisco on 9 March 1951, belongs to the first squadron to receive the first production F3D-1s. (SDAM via Mark Aldrich)

An F3D-1 of VMF(N)-542 soars over MCAS El Toro, California, in 1951. The squadron trained Marine pilots and radar operators for eventual duty with VMF(N)-513 in Korea where the squadron's F3D-2 Skyknights downed six enemy aircraft. (Mark Aldrich)

The Marine Corps selected VMF(N)-542 in late 1951 to train personnel on the F3D-1 Skyknight for eventual deployment to Korea. This aircraft, BuNo 123767, was the second to last F3D-1 produced before Douglas switched production over to the F3D-2. (SDAM via Mark Aldrich)

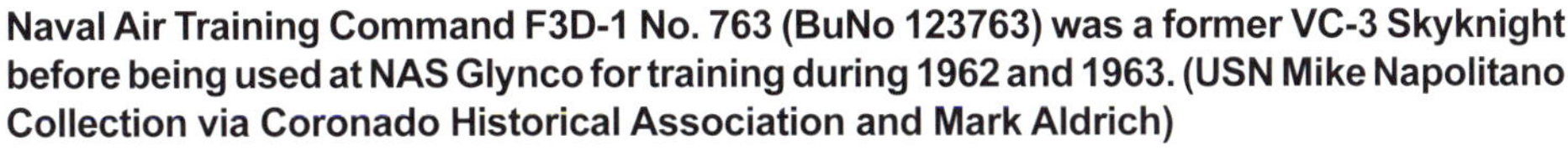

Naval Air Training Command F3D-1 No. 763 (BuNo 123763) was a former VC-3 Skyknight before being used at NAS Glynco for training during 1962 and 1963. (USN Mike Napolitano Collection via Coronado Historical Association and Mark Aldrich)

Throughout the 1950s, a number of F3D-1 Skyknights tested missiles at China Lake Naval Ordnance Test Station (NOTS) – renamed Naval Weapons Center (NWC) – and at Pt. Mugu. BuNo 123757, shown here with a Sidewinder-1 air-to-air missile at China Lake on 6 November 1952, participated in a several such tests. (U.S. Navy via Gary Verver)

Three F3D Skyknights take part in tests at China Lake on 1 August 1953. In the foreground, F3D-1 BuNos 123767 and 123757 are fitted with AIM-9A Sidewinder-1 missiles, while the F3D-2 BuNo 124595 in the rear is carrying a T-63 simulator for the Mk-7 nuclear bomb. (U.S. Navy via Gary Verver)

Fitted with sidewinder missiles, BuNo 123757 wings its way over southern California on 11 December 1952. This aircraft was struck off record at MCAS Cherry Point in February 1964. (U.S. Navy via Gary Verver)

Lacking a tailhook, F3D-1 BuNo 123757 has been loaded with a Sidewinder EX-0 missile on the right and a "target" five-inch HVAR rocket on the left on 18 May 1953. The HVAR was fired first and then the Sidewinder was then launched to track it. The aircraft displays day-glo orange wing panels, white codes, and double red bands around the rear engine nacelles. (U.S. Navy via Gary Verver)

BuNo 123744 fires a Sidewinder missile over fumaroles in California on 18 March 1958. This Skyknight was placed in storage Litchfield Park a year later and scrapped. (U.S. Navy via Gary Verver)

An AIM-9B Sidewinder missile is mounted on F3D-1 BuNo 123744 at China Lake on 20 November 1958. This Skyknight, wearing the gray and white coloration adopted by the Navy in 1958, was scrapped at Litchfield Park in May 1959. (U.S. Navy via Gary Verver)

Packing Sidewinder missiles, China Lake F3D-1 Skyknight BuNo 123744 and F3H-2N Demon BuNo 133550 cruise over fumaroles in Long Valley Caldera, California, on 18 March 1958. (U.S. Navy via Gary Verver)

A civilian technician stands next to a Radioplane XKD4R-1 target drone mounted on an F3D-1M, possibly BuNo 123747, at China Lake in 1958. The term "Woodson's Klooge" is hand written on the bottom portion of the mount. (U.S. Navy via Gary Verver)

F3D-1M

The F3D-1M, fitted with two hardpoints underneath the inboard and outboard wing panels, was used to test the Sparrow I air-to-air missile at China Lake and Point Mugu. Successful missile testing of F3D-1 aircraft evolved into the modification of the second Skyknight prototype BuNo 121458 and F3D-1 BuNo 123748. Both aircraft performed field firing tests under Task 13 of the XAAM-N-2 Sparrow Development Program in conjunction with the Bureau of Aeronautics and Sperry Gyroscope Company, Division of The Sperry Corporation. BuNo 123748 was equipped with a partial AN/APQ-36 system. It is not known if the XF3D was actually equipped with a functioning fire-control radar. The Douglas Aircraft Company took part in the task under a subcontract. Task 13 was initiated June 1950 and extended to August 1952. Field testing was completed in December 1951. The manufacturing of test equipment under Task 13 continued until August 1952. The prototype at Point Mugu was fitted with an accessory panel to control missile firing and a Fastax camera to record missile separation and launch. Launches of dummy and live missiles were conducted from altitudes of 500 to 20,000 feet.

The Navy's first intercept by a Sparrow I radar beam-riding missile was an F6F drone hit by the XF3D-1M on 3 December 1952. Twelve F3D-1Ms were produced (BuNos 123741, 123743, 123746, 123747, 123748, 123749, 123750, 123751, 123754, 123756, 123758, and 123760) and operated by VX-4 and VX-5 from Point Mugu and China Lake. Those still in service were designated as the MF-10A in 1962. The successful tests of the -1M led to the development of the F3D-2M.

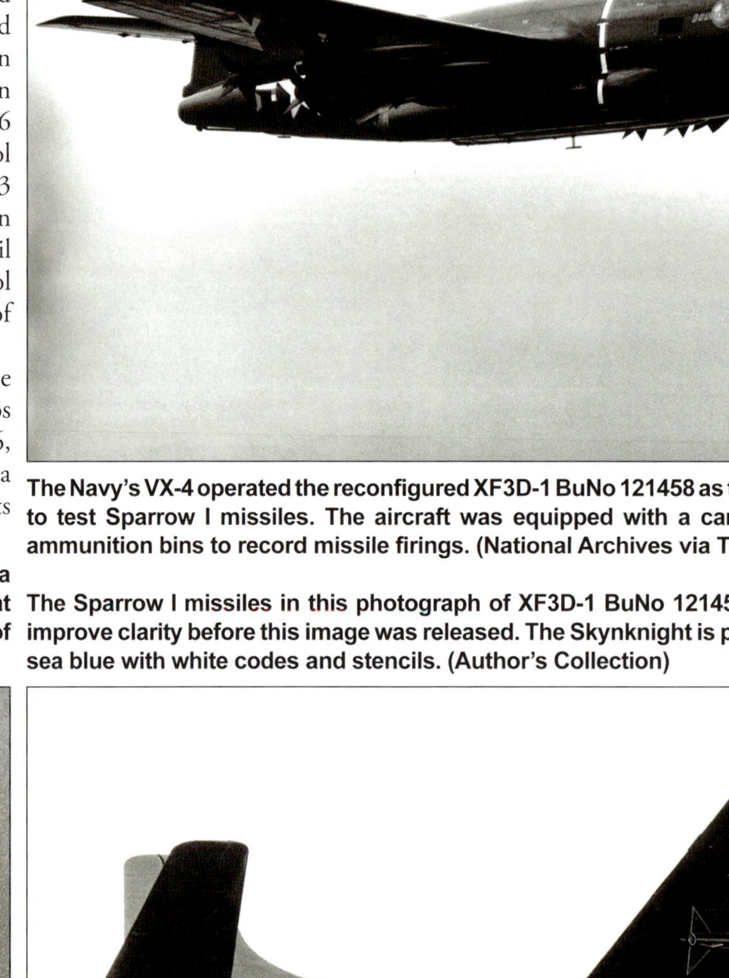

The Navy's VX-4 operated the reconfigured XF3D-1 BuNo 121458 as the F3D-1M prototype to test Sparrow I missiles. The aircraft was equipped with a camera installed in the ammunition bins to record missile firings. (National Archives via Tommy H. Thomason)

Point Mugu-based F3D-1M BuNo 123758 with overall glossy sea blue coloring fires a Sparrow missile. This aircraft was one of a dozen production F3D-1 Skyknights that carried the -1M designation. Successful evaluation of the -1M led to the production of the F3D-2M. (Rich Dann)

The Sparrow I missiles in this photograph of XF3D-1 BuNo 121458 were retouched to improve clarity before this image was released. The Skynknight is painted overall glossy sea blue with white codes and stencils. (Author's Collection)

F3D-1M, BuNo 123758, in 1958 with a Sparrow 2 under the wing with a camera housed in the ammunition bin to document missile testing. Like most of her sisters, this aircraft probably went to Litchfield Park for disposal during the early 1960s. (Rich Dann)

F3D-2

The F3D-1's inability to reach expected high-speed performance compelled the Navy to issue a new set of specifications on 23 May 1949. Again, Douglas sought increased performance using Westinghouse J46-WE-3 afterburner turbojets. Other improvements with the F3D-2 included forward armor protection, consisting of a 70-pound plate and a 105-pound flak-resistant windshield of armor glass; a spoiler system to permit a higher roll rate; the General Electric G-3 autopilot; and improved air conditioning. The tail-warning radar, located in the aft fuselage, gave a Skyknight crew an advantage in being able to detect approaching enemy aircraft from the rear. The system monitored astern, side-by-side, and up-and-down in a 70-degree sweep radius and had a maximum range of four miles. The addition of the APS-28 became invaluable over the skies of North Korea, as it alerted Skyknight crews of Soviet-built MiG fighters attempting to sneak up behind the American night fighter.

The Navy ordered the F3D-2 in August 1949, with the first of the aircraft flying on 14 February 1951 but without the J46 power plant. The installation of the upgraded engines never materialized and all 221 F3D-2 units (BuNos 124595 through 124664, BuNos 125783 through 125882, and BuNos 127019 through 127085) utilized the J34-WE-36/36A turbojets with 3,400 pounds of thrust each. The number also included 16 missile-equipped F3D-2Ms. The dash-36 engines slightly improved the aircraft's performance but not to the extent that the J46s would have, and thus the Skyknight's high-speed capability never reached the full potential envisioned by Douglas and the Navy. The performance characteristics for the F3D-2 were: speed 580 m.p.h. at sea level and 493 m.p.h. at 35,000 feet; service ceiling 38,200 feet and a range of 1,375 miles with internal and external fuel stores. Initial rate of climb was 3,700 feet per minute.

NACA engineers at the Lewis Flight Propulsion Laboratory in Cleveland, Ohio, and pilots of the F3D-2 found faults with the engine's compressor blades, the location of the engines in relation to the aircraft's ground clearance, and the inadequacy of the engines to provide sufficient power.

While the Skyknight was in service during the Korean War there was speculation that engine-compressor blade failure of the J34WE-36 possibly caused the loss of four Skyknights and the deaths of their flight crews, including two from the Navy's VC-4 and possibly another pair from the Marine's VMF(N)-513. During a training flight in 1952, an engine on an F3D-2 belonging to VC-4 threw compressor blades into the fuel tank, setting the aircraft ablaze. Fortunately, the pilot, Lt. Glen L. Wegener, managed to land successfully at NAS Atlantic City.

The crew of another VC-4 Skyknight were not as lucky. VC-4 detachment commander, Lt Cdr. Howard L. Terry, and his RO Petty Officer Howard A. O'Neil were killed just after Terry had lifted his aircraft off the runway at NAS Atlantic City in heavy rain and fog on the evening of 18 March 1953. The F3D cleared the ground but then crashed just a mile-and-a-half from the airfield.

Parked on the ground by the paint shed at Douglas El Segundo in about 1952 or 1953, F3D-2 BuNo 127059 sports the words DOUGLAS F3D SKYNIGHT applied to the nose but lacks unit codes. (Tailhook Association via Clay Jansson)

NAS Atlantic City-based VC-4 NA/602, BuNo 124646, and NA/603, BuNo 124647, fly above the clouds in mid-1953. NA/603 was later converted to an Electronic Warfare (EW) F3D-2Q and served in VMCJ-2 at MCAS Cherry Point, North Carolina. The aircraft crashed after an engine flameout in May 1958. (Tailhook Association)

NATC BuNo 124611 became one of the original F3D-2 carrier test aircraft. It went on to serve with VMF(N)-513 and was later reconfigured as an F3D-2T2 for training radar operators. (SDAM via Mark Aldrich)

With a first series F3D-2, BuNo 124634, behind him, Douglas engineer Ed Heinemann receives the keys of a new 1953 Olds Super 88 Deluxe at the Douglas Aircraft Factory. (SDAM via Mark Aldrich)

A McDonnell F2H-3(4) and F2H-2 fly along with an F3D-2 of VC-3 in 1952. The squadron operated a variety of Naval aircraft during the 1950s. (USN and Bill Knutson via Tailhook Association)

Seen here still without unit codes in about 1951, BuNo 127038 was delivered from the factory to the Navy as the first F3D-2M and may have operated with VF-11 at some later date. (SDAM via Mark Aldrich)

Parked at an undisclosed location on 17 May 1952, this first series -2 test aircraft BuNo 124604 has the period glossy sea blue coloring, white codes and matching blue wheel rims. (Author's Collection)

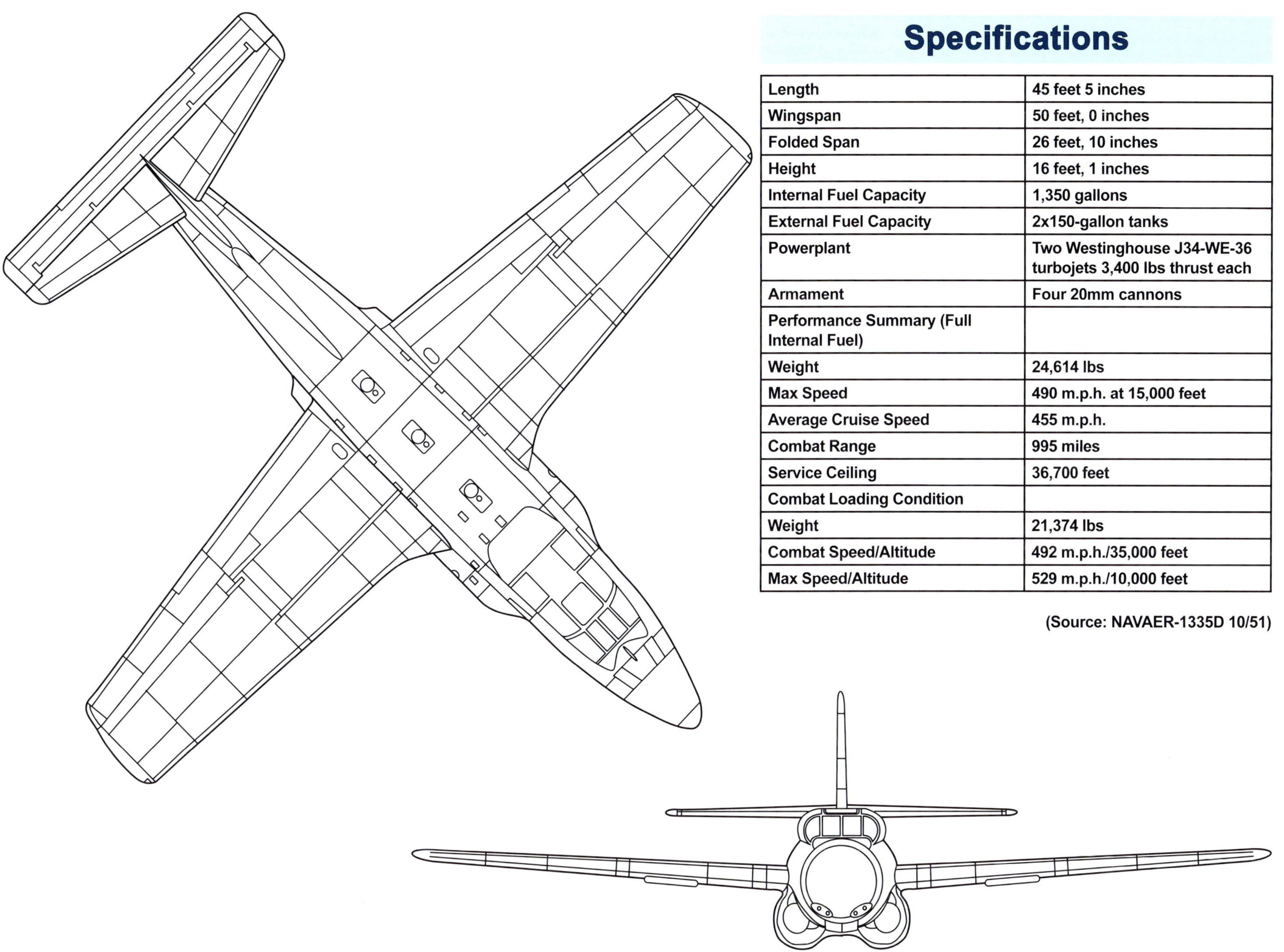

Specifications

Length	45 feet 5 inches
Wingspan	50 feet, 0 inches
Folded Span	26 feet, 10 inches
Height	16 feet, 1 inches
Internal Fuel Capacity	1,350 gallons
External Fuel Capacity	2x150-gallon tanks
Powerplant	Two Westinghouse J34-WE-36 turbojets 3,400 lbs thrust each
Armament	Four 20mm cannons
Performance Summary (Full Internal Fuel)	
Weight	24,614 lbs
Max Speed	490 m.p.h. at 15,000 feet
Average Cruise Speed	455 m.p.h.
Combat Range	995 miles
Service Ceiling	36,700 feet
Combat Loading Condition	
Weight	21,374 lbs
Combat Speed/Altitude	492 m.p.h./35,000 feet
Max Speed/Altitude	529 m.p.h./10,000 feet

(Source: NAVAER-1335D 10/51)

Korean War

Marine training with the Skyknight for service in the Korean War began with the reorganization of Marine Night Fighter Squadrons 513 and 542 in late February 1952. VMF(N)-513 had conducted combat operations in Korea since August 1950, flying the F4U-5N, while VMF(N)-542 began missions in September of that year with the F7F-3N. In late February 1952, VMF(N)-542 personnel not integrated into -513 returned to El Toro MCAS, California. There, on 24 March they began orientation on the Skyknight. Initial training began with the F3D-1, but it was soon replaced by the -2 model and training was completed by late May.

After the training period, 15 F3Ds flew to San Diego on 1 June and were loaded onto the U.S.S. *Windham Bay* (TCVE-92). The aircraft arrived in Japan on 18 June, and aircraft, personnel, and equipment showed up at Itami airfield, Japan, between 18 and 22 June 1952. Col. Peter D. Lambrecht led the first flight of four Skyknights to Kunsan Airbase on 24 June with another eight aircraft arriving by the 27th with Lambrecht assuming command of the squadron upon his arrival. The squadron now operated three different types of aircraft: the F4U-5N, F7F-3N, and the F3D-2. In the months to come, the number of war-weary Corsairs and Tigercats would dwindle until the Skyknight became the squadron's only tactical aircraft. The arrival of the F3D in Korea changed VMF(N)-513's primary mission from close air support and interdiction missions to protecting Air

Force B-26 and B-29 bombers from MiG fighters during night raids over North Korea. Although such missions were flown by USAF squadrons, VMF(N)-513 was the first and only Marine jet night fighter squadron to be assigned the task of protecting friendly bombers. In the capable hands of of a pilot and RO, the Skyknight proved its worth by scoring the highest number of aerial victories for an all-weather fighter in Korea.

VMF(N)-513's inventory of aircraft in early July 1952 consisted of 12 F3D-2s, 12 F7F-3Ns, and six F4U-5Ns. By the end of the month, however, none of the Skyknights was combat ready and they would not become completely operational for nearly four months, due to a lack of parts, maintenance issues, and the loss of two of the jets. Initially, the jets were restricted to flying only training and familiarity flights, as the squadron waited for the arrival of 20mm gun barrel extensions, without which the outgoing rounds could damage the aircraft. A second issue was the short life of the APS-35 radar system's vacuum tubes, which accounted for a 75-percent failure rate of the equipment, compounded by an inadequate supply of spares. The barrel extensions arrived and were installed on the squadron's complement of Skyknights by the second week of August and the first scheduled operational flight began on 11th with a night combat air patrol (NCAP) near Cho-do Island. Five days after operations resumed, the commanding officer, Col. Lambrecht, and his radar operator Lt. James M. Brown failed to return from a patrol while flying BuNo 124623 on the 15th. A subsequent search failed to locate the aircraft and its crew was listed as MIA. The loss of Lambrecht's aircraft did not raise any concerns

WF/3 landing at Kimpo Air Base in 1953 with a C-46 cargo plane in the background. Detachments of VMF(N)-513 Skyknights, along with squadron's Grumman F7F-3N Tigercats and F4U-5N Corsairs, were often sent up to Kimpo on the outskirts of Seoul to counter North Korean aircraft sent to harass UN positions located in and around the city. (Author's Collection)

from a maintenance standpoint but the loss of a second Skyknight a month later raised the possibility that both F3Ds were lost due to catastrophic engine failure. Jet operations were restricted to test flights during September when BuNo 124625 piloted by Maj. Harrold J.Eiland with radar operator MSgt. Alois A.Motil crashed soon after take-off.

In a statement given by MSgt. Motil to crash investigators, the aircraft apparently suffered a catastrophic turbine-blade failure. Prior to departing the crew noticed the starboard engine took an excessive long time to start. Halfway down the runway both engines briefly lost rpm but they returned to normal as the aircraft lifted off, something neither of the crew had experienced before. The fighter made a normal climb until four minutes into the flight when the Skyknight suffered catastrophic engine failure.

"At what I thought to be 3,000 feet altitude, we experienced an explosion in the starboard engine accompanied by a blinding light…and a clanging noise indicative of metal on metal. When the right wing dropped, the pilot took corrective action. Immediately thereafter, a second explosion took place, this time in the left engine. As I turned my head to the radar scope, we experienced a third blinding explosion at which time I could feel the tail of the aircraft come up violently, similar to a somersault," Motil testified. The aircraft then crashed and a crash boat subsequently picked up MSgt. Motil but the body of Maj. Eiland was not recovered. Results of an investigative report theorized

that rotor blade loading in the third stage of the engine compressor may have played a critical part in Maj. Eiland's crash and possibly that of Col. Lambrecht. By mid-October, the squadron engineered a quick fix by applying armor plating, called a compressor shield fabricated from rolled steel plating, around the compressor engine housing.

The F3D-2 scored the highest number of kills for a jet night fighter during the Korean War, with VMF(N)-513 scoring six confirmed victories over piston and turbojet aircraft between November 1952 and January 1953. Maj. William T. Stratton with his RO MSgt. Hans Hoglind became the first F3D team to score a victory at night against an enemy jet on 3 November 1952. At 0107 hours while the Skyknight cruised at 14,000 feet, Hoglind established radar contact with an unidentified aircraft at a distance of seven miles. Contact was temporarily lost but soon reestablished and Stratton closed to 2,100 feet. The APG-26 would not lock on, but the crew made a visual sighting on a Soviet built Yak-17, originally identified as a Yak-15, jet interceptor three minutes after initial contact. Stratton fired three bursts of 20-mm fire at 12,000 feet altitude, approximately 1,200 feet behind the enemy aircraft. The first burst hit the port wing of the Yak, a second hit the fuselage, and a third entered the tail pipe. The aircraft went down on fire.

During the night of 8 November 1952, Capt. Oliver R. Davis and his RO W/O Dramus F. Fessler were assigned to a Night Combat Air Patrol (NCAP) mission to work

WF-9, possibly BuNo 127030, at an undisclosed location in Korea in about 1953, lacks a tail hook and bumper. The Marines were not too happy with the aircraft's performance since it was well below what had been predicted. VMF(N)-513 removed the tail hook and bumper from nine F3Ds and kept records to see if the lighter weight improved performance. (SDAM via Mark Aldrich)

with "Dutchboy," the call sign of one of the Ground-Controlled Intercept (GCI) stations. At 0132 hours, Dutchboy vectored the F3D to a bogey at a distance of 10 miles, flying at 12,000 feet. "I began a dive from 19,500 feet and added full power at 14,000 feet," Davis recalled. RO, Warrant Officer Fessler established contact and ordered a gentle starboard turn. "Contact was lost immediately and I requested further help from Dutchboy," said Davis. Dutchboy vectored him on a new heading and his RO reestablished contact with the bogey flying at their 12 o'clock at a range of three miles. He ordered a gentle turn to starboard and Davis executed a 30-degree bank. He later remembered: "We began closing at an indicated airspeed of 450 knots. My RO placed us in a position where the bogey was 10 degrees starboard, three miles, at 12,000 feet. As we closed, I got a visual on a jet exhaust. I requested Dutchboy to distinguish as to whether it was a bogey or a bandit. He replied, 'Bag it!' 'Bag it!'"

By then the Skyknight was closing to within a quarter-to-half-a-mile of the enemy's exhaust. "I momentarily popped speed breaks. The exhaust was so bright it was hard for me to make out the airframe outline. The bandit began a hard starboard turn. I turned with him and fired a short burst of about 20 rounds of 20mm into the tail pipe." There was a large explosion and parts flew past Davis' aircraft. "I was closing dangerously. I pulled hard back on the stick and since I was already in a hard starboard turn, I passed the enemy to the right. I observed flames and black smoke passing from the center portion of his plane. After reversing my turn, I picked up a visual of the flaming craft as it descended and crashed. I opened fire at 0136 and the plane crashed at 0137," Davis said.

The next aerial kill for The Flying Nightmares was a first for Marine aviation when an F3D, flown by 1stLt. Joseph A. Corvi and MSgt. Dan R. George, destroyed a PO-2 at night using only the APS-26 gun tracking radar. At 1935 hours on 10 December 1952, ground control at Cho-do vectored the orbiting Skyknight into position for an interception. George picked up and locked onto the bandit with the APS-26 radar at a range of one-and-a-half miles. Range was reduced to 1,000 yards astern of the enemy and was guided exclusively by the APS-26 when Corvi opened fire at an altitude of 2,000 feet. A three-second burst followed and the radar screen's pipper (the dot indicating the target) began to fluctuate and then disappear. Lt. Corvi broke off the chase. Corvi looked up from his scope and outside saw three burning pieces of the enemy aircraft falling out of the sky.

The F3D's crew watched as the PO-2 twisted and turned until it fell into the water. GCI notified Corvi that another "low and slow" bandit was moving in an adjoining area. Sgt. George picked up the new bogey at 2,500 feet on his APD-21. The Skyknight's pilot executed a turn and came around on a stern position of the approaching plane. Again, the APG-26 locked on and Corvi opened fire at a range of 1,100 yards. The radar's pip fluctuated as before and the target disappeared, but destruction of the second North Korean heckler could not be confirmed as no debris was seen by the aircrew.

The last three air-to-air kills by VMF(N)-513 occurred in January 1953 during the course of protecting B-29 bombers hitting targets in North Korea. The typical escort mission involved upwards of nine F3D-2 aircraft, with two serving as spares, assigned to cover an 18-plane B-29 strike on a bridge complex in the Anju-Sinanju area. The bombers utilized Shoran to locate and strike their targets. The B-29s struck in two streams of nine

WF/7 in overall flat black and red codes prepares to depart from an unknown location in South Korea in about 1952 for an NCAP in support of USAF B-29 Supefortress strikes against North Korean and Chinese targets. (SDAM via Mark Aldrich)

A pair of VMF(N)-513 Skyknights depart an unidentified airfield in Korea in about 1952. In the foreground is one of the squadron's complement of F7F-3N Tigercats that were replaced as additional Skyknights arrived in theater. (SDAM via Mark Aldrich)

aircraft each, with a brief interval of one minute between each aircraft and with the lead aircraft of each strike having the same time on target. Each element would utilize a different IP (Initial Point), and would transmit a code word indicating when the bombers had passed each point. The flight leader of the night fighters would inform the flight leader of the B-29s when the F3Ds were on station.

The F3Ds would be tactically disposed in the following manner. Two aircraft, the barrier CAP, would fly to a pre-selected area controlled by GCI in order to block any effort by the enemy to send fighters into the bomber stream. A fourth Skyknight would be the target CAP and served as the escort leader. His job was to watch the bombers go through the target area and block any attempted interception at this, the most vulnerable point of the flight, since the enemy utilized a searchlight and fighter coordination network; the Soviet-built interceptors flown by Soviet, North Korean People's Army (NKPA), and Chinese Communist (CHICOM) pilots were not equipped with radar intercept systems. Additional Skyknights, usually two, rendezvoused with each stream at their Initial Point and escorted them to the target, flying a racetrack pattern above and around the stream, while keeping them under radar surveillance. Similarly, another set of F3Ds provided a protective umbrella to each bomber stream above the target area and escorted the B-29s away from the area after completion of the bomb run.

In addition, at least two spare Skyknights would be airborne and held in the vicinity of the target, enabling the night flight leader to replace any aircraft that might develop radar or mechanical problems. After the bomber leader confirmed that none of his B-29s was damaged or missing, he notified the night fighter leader and the F3Ds were released

Internal stores of 20mm ammunition for the nose cannons were loaded into bins below the rear cockpit area.

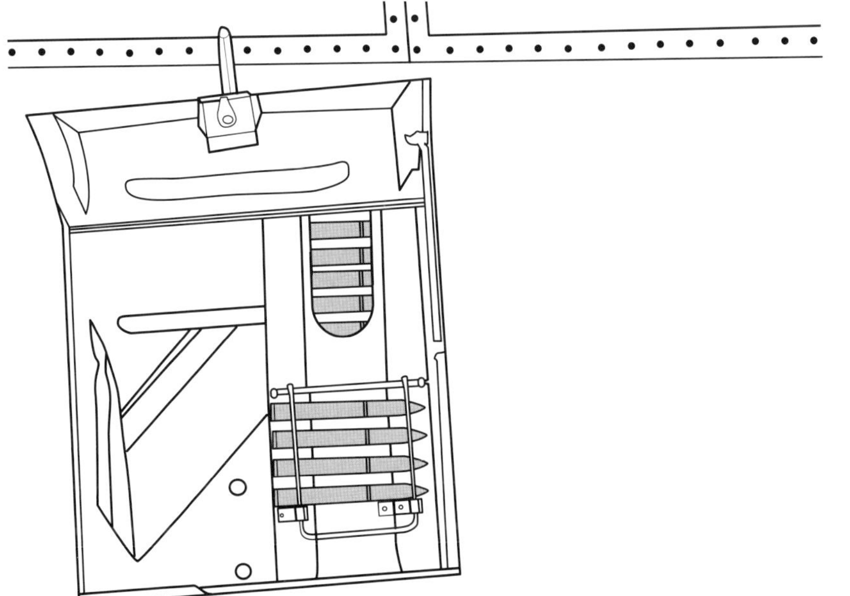

The installation of 150-gallon drop tanks mounted on inboard wing mounts would extend the combat range of the Skyknight. (SDAM via Mark Aldrich)

The Skyknight could carry a maximum of 4,000 pounds of bombs and 11.75-inch rockets. VMF(N)-513 did conduct a few close air support strikes with bomb-laden F3Ds in 1953. (SDAM via Mark Aldrich)

and returned to base.

The typical B-29 escort mission over North Korea often resulted in contacts with enemy aircraft and close calls supplemented by the occasional victory over MiGs attempting to intercept and shoot down either a bomber or an escorting night fighter. Sometimes, the night fighters were too late in intercepting the tenacious MiG-15s bent on bringing down an American bomber, as was the case on the evening of 30 December 1952.

Two F3Ds piloted by Lt. Col. Robert F. Conley and Capt. Oliver Davis with the call signs Enrage 3387 and 3388 flew escort for B-29s of the Nineteenth Bomb Group, Twenty-Eighth Bomber Squadron, on a strike against an ore processing plant northwest of North Korea's capital of Pyongyang. Peering through the darkness Capt. Davis was looking for his second aerial victory since downing a MiG-15 on 8 November. Shaking off a probing North Korean searchlight Davis and his RO Warrant Officer Dramus Fessler proceeded to the planned orbit point at 30,000 feet. Four minutes after arriving, he heard a B-29 pilot over the radio saying he was under fighter attack. Capt. Davis turned westward and within two minutes saw one of the bombers caught in approximately 10 searchlights 20 miles ahead, and under attack by an enemy fighter. Closing in, Davis heard the bomber pilot saying that his aircraft was hit and on fire, with the number-four engine feathered. The F3D crew made a visual sighting of the stricken bomber and Davis proceeded at maximum speed on a westerly heading. The Skyknight picked up another radio transmission from a different bomber saying it too was under attack. Davis turned

north, tracked, identified, and began following a burning B-29 as its pilot radioed that his crew were bailing out. Two minutes later, Davis and Fessler saw the big B-29 crash 25 miles north of Pyongyang. Two other B-29s sustained heavy damage from the enemy jets but managed to make it back to Suwon, although neither of them flew again. The MiGs won the night but three of them would fall to Skyknights in January 1953.

Four F3Ds departed Kunsan airfield beginning at 2035 hours on 12 January to escort B-29s to Sinanju. Maj. E. P. "Jack" Dunn and MSgt. Lawrence J. Fortin took off at 2105 hours and picked up the bombers forty minutes later. TDAC alerted the F3D about an approaching bandit. MSgt. Lawrence picked it up on his screen about 10 miles heading directly for North Korean searchlights over the B-29s' target area. Maj. Dunn descended to the same altitude as the bombers and contact with the bandit was lost for 15 minutes. The Skyknight's radar picked up another contact at 10 miles and Maj. Dunn went in for an intercept. "We closed to four-and-a-half miles and got a visual on an aircraft that had a white light on each wing tip. The plane was flying north to south, about five miles west of Sinanju at a speed estimated in excess of 500 knots. I was flying at 20,000 feet at the time, the bandit appearing to be about 5,000 feet below," said Dunn. Maj. Dunn called TDAC to confirm whether there were any friendly aircraft around and ground control reported none in the area. By this time the bandit had turned northeast over the searchlights at Sinanju and turned off its wing lights, it was soon identified as a MiG-15. Unknown to the Skyknight crew, the MiG was serving as a decoy to lure American night fighters over

The nose cone of WF/7 is opened for Marine technicians to check the voltage on the aircraft's electronic systems. Not known for superior speed, it relied on its intercept and tail-warning radar to detect enemy aircraft. (NMNA)

Marine ordnance men load WF/7 with 20mm ammunition for the aircraft's four nose-mounted cannons via a compartment located below the bulkhead. Each of the Skyknight's cannons held a capacity of 200 rounds of ammunition. (NMNA)

the searchlights and anti-aircraft guns.

The MiG pilot lured the Skyknight over the gun batteries as bursts of anti-aircraft shells bracketed Maj. Dunn's aircraft but the F3D's RO continued to track the enemy aircraft, giving his pilot course corrections as the MiG flew in and out of the searchlights at 10,000 feet. "The bandit made a turn back into the searchlights. This turn enabled us to close more rapidly on him and after about five minutes of this figure-eight turning, we obtained a lock-on with our APG-26 gear. I opened fire and let go approximately six bursts. I saw what appeared to be a fire coming from the aircraft," Dunn said. The pilot of the bandit turned his lights off and made a left turn over the searchlights. Dunn continued, "He was in a climbing left turn when my RO obtained another lock-on for me. I opened fire and, almost immediately, he burst into flames. He continued his climbing left turn with the fire increasing. His plane then nosed over and crashed."

The squadron scored its last two kills within two days of each other at the end of January. On 28 January, Capt. James R. Weaver and MSgt. Robert P. Becker claimed another MiG-15 kill during a bomber escort mission. The Skyknight was inbound at 30,000 feet to position itself between the first and second bomber streams. On the return leg after the B-29s had hit targets at Sinuiju, ground control on Cho-do Island told Capt. Weaver of a bandit closing in from 20 miles. The aircraft disappeared from ground control two minutes later. A second bandit appeared on Becker's scope at a range of seven miles and the night fighter dropped down to intercept and engage. The enemy fighter was flying fast and low at an altitude of 1,300 feet, slightly to port and below the incoming Marine night fighter. Weaver fired four or five three-second bursts at a range of 1,500

feet and saw two puffs of smoke and flames coming from the center fuselage as the MiG plummeted to earth.

Three days later Lt. Col. Robert Conley and his R/O MSgt. James M. Scott made the last MiG-15 kill, the tenth and last air-to-air victory for The Flying Nightmares while on another escort mission. The night fighter had been airborne for 45 minutes when ground control reported multiple bandits heading for the B-29s. Scott's radar picked up one of the bandits at a range of six miles and Conley began descending while applying 100-percent power. The Skyknight quickly closed the range to less than two miles but Scott could not get a lock-on with the APG-26. However, it was a clear night and the crew visually picked up the enemy aircraft slightly below and silhouetted by the moon. Col. Conley opened fire from a distance of 2,400 feet as the F3D fell behind the MiG and continued to fire bursts as range closed to within 1,000 feet. The F3D passed over the stricken jet and Conley, while making a 360-degree turn, lost track of the MiG, but noticed a fire blazing atop a snow-capped mountain below them.

A detachment of five crews and four F3D-2s from VC-4, known as The Nightcappers, based on the USS *Lake Champlain* (CV-39) joined 513 at K-6 airbase at Pyongtaek on 21 June 1953. It was during VC-4's deployment with the Marine night fighter squadron the Nightcappers lost its only F3D-2 and crew, possibly due to enemy action. Lt. (jg) Robert "Bob" Bick and his RO Chief Petty Officer (CPO) Linton Smith were on a routine NCAP near Cho-do before dawn on 2 July when Bick called ground control radar about a possible bogey that Smith had detected on his scope. Bick asked permission to fire but Cho-do ground control could not confirm the bogey and told Bick to wait.

Maintenance personnel of VMF(N)-513 work on the landing gear of an unknown Skyknight at a Korean airfield in about 1953. A considerable amount of the aircraft's undercoating is showing through. (USMC)

Major Elswin P. (Jack) Dunn (left) and MSgt. Larry Fortin of (N)-513 pose in front of a squadron F3D-2 Skyknight in Korea. Dunn was credited with a MiG kill on 12 January 1953. (Emil Buehler Library, NMNA)

VC-4 Douglas F3D-2 NA/603, BuNo 127022, seen in the air in April 1953, was one of a four-plane detachment from the USS *Lake Champlain* that operated in Korea during the summer of 1953. (Emil Buehler Library NMNA)

VC-4 NA/74, BuNo 124645, rests on the tarmac at Atlantic City, New Jersey, in 1952. The unit sent one detachment to Korea for duty with VMF(N)-513. This aircraft had a long operational history with its last combat assignment with VMCJ-1 in Vietnam. (NMNA)

Bick asked permission once more but did not get the clearance to shoot the suspected MiG-15. Moments later, he called Cho-do, stating he had fired on the unidentified aircraft, possibly destroying it, but his aircraft had sustained damage from 37mm cannon fire and he was returning to base. Soon thereafter, ground control lost radar and radio contact with the F3D as it headed south. Lt. Bick's loss was likely due to a new tactic adopted by the Communists to battle the F3D-2s prowling over North Korea, since their interceptors lacked onboard radar equipment. It may have also caused the downing of a Marine Skyknight flown by Capt. James B. Brown and Sgt. James V. "Red" Harrell who failed to return to Kunsan Airfield from a mission on 30 May. Evidence of their fate turned up in 2001 when a South Korean family found the dog tags and remains of Harrell on a beach near Kunsan. One source lists Chinese People's Liberation Army Air Force (PLAAF) pilot Hou Shujun as shooting down the Skyknight, but Marine Corps records do not corroborate this account.

Although Communist forces lacked fighters with airborne radar, they did have above-average ground-based radar systems and used them effectively to guide MiGs towards American aircraft. Orbiting MiGs, typically four to six aircraft, would wait until their own GCI picked up an American night fighter, and ground control would attempt to jam communication between the night fighter and friendly GCI stations. Meanwhile, the flight of MiGs, in radio contact with their own ground control, would send one of their own as bait for the American aircraft. The search radar on the patrolling F3D-2s would pick up the approaching enemy and then seek an intercept. When a Skyknight came within range of its gun-laying radar, the other MiGs flying at a lower altitude would vector towards the night fighter guided by their GCI. To keep the Americans focused on their target, the bait-aircraft would flash a strobe light. If the radar operator wasn't paying close attention to the aircraft's tail warning radar, the incoming MiGs would attempt a rear attack for a kill. This ploy may have resulted in the last loss suffered by The Flying Nightmares when F3D-2 Capt. L. Thistlethwaite and RO SSgt. W. H. Westbrook went MIA while on combat air patrol on 4 July 1953 near the same area where Lt. Bick and CPO Smith of VC-4 had been lost.

On a few occasions, Skyknights provided close air support when other air assets were unavailable. Combat over Korea for Navy and Marine night fighter crews ended with Skyknights providing close air support from 19 to 26 July during vicious battles between UN and CHICOM forces over a defensive complex named Berlin and East Berlin initially held by the Marines, then the Chinese, and ending with the Marines retaking the positions. VMF(N)-513 lost five Skyknights (three to operational accidents and two to enemy action) and seven crewmembers, while VC-4, as mentioned earlier, lost one aircraft and crew.

VMF(N)-513, later designated as VMF(AW)-513, continued to operate the F3D-2 from bases in Korea and Japan through the 1950s and became a guided-missile squadron in 1959 when the squadron received missile-carrying F3D-2Ms from VMF(AW)-542 in 1959. During the F3D-2's military service life, Douglas and the Navy converted well over 100 of the variant to the either the F3D-2B, F3D-2M, F3D-2T2, or F3D-2Q configuration with the Navy and Marines operating the aircraft units until June 1970.

A sign at K-6 airfield at Pyongtaek, South Korea, circa winter 1953-54 shows the date of departure from the U.S. and base assignments in Korea from July 1950 to June 1953. The stars at the bottom show the number of air-to-air kills. (Emil Buehler Library NMNA)

A pilot and radar officer from VMF(N)-513 in Korea at K-4 airfield with squadron Skyknights in background. Both are wearing the rubber-lined "poopy" anti-exposure suit. (Eugene S. "Mule" Holmburg via Tailhook Association)

Seen in profile at K-3 Pohang airbase is $12\frac{7}{8}$ BuNo 127027. The number $12\frac{7}{8}$ was the closest number to "unlucky 13" that a VMF(N)-513 crew wanted to have in Korea. (NMNA)

A pair of airmen stand next to this *12⅞* in about 1954. The considerable amount of mud on the engine nacelle and wing was due to Pohang airfield's often wet conditions. (Tom Doll via Rich Dunn)

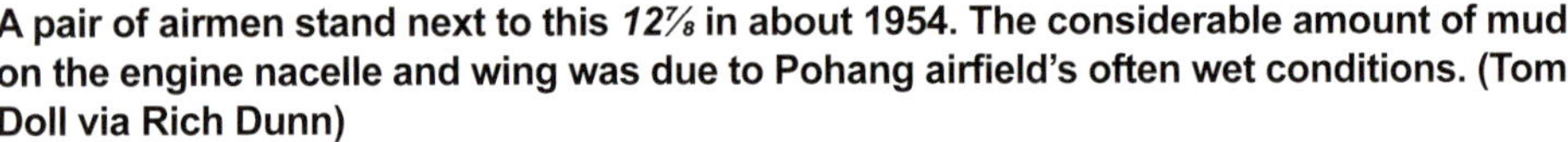

Flying out of K-6 with speed brakes deployed in about 1954, WF *12⅞*, shows a considerable amount of paint wear on the wing. Engine exhaust has also stained the fuselage. (Eugene S. "Mule" Holmburg via Tailhook Association)

Radar operator SSgt. Eugene "Mule" Holmberg of 513s at Pohang (K-3) in 1953 wears typical flight garb of the period. Behind him stands the squadron's complement of F3D-2 aircraft. (Emil Buehler Library, NMNA)

Marine personnel smile for the camera during the winter of 1953-1954 at Kunsan AB, South Korea. Behind them are three of the squadron's Skyknights with possibly BuNo 127059 in the foreground. (Emil Buehler Library, NMNA)

Maintenance is being performed on the AN/APQ-35 radar systems of two of VMF(N)-513s Skyknights. WF/6 has the earlier sea blue coloration while WF/21 in the background appears to have the overall flat black. (Jay Miller Collection via Tommy H. Thomason)

Wearing their exposure suits, two VMF(N)-513 members, pilot Donald Harvey (left) and SSGT Dave Upchurch (RO), pose next to WF/8 at K-6 Korea in 1955. Right of the number 8 is the name *Toni.* (Eugene S. "Mule" Holmburg via Tailhook Association Collection)

A pair of F3D-2s of VMF(N)-513 form up over Korea in late 1953 or early 1954. WF/8 shows considerable wear around the port engine intake area, possibly due to the ground grew climbing onto the engine nacelle to reach an access panel.

Well-worn VMF(N)-513 F3D-2 WF/24 shows its undercoat in a flight out of K-6 in Korea in 1955. The weathering has obscured the aircraft's bureau number. (Eugene S. "Mule" Holmburg via The Tailhook Association Collection)

WF-12, not *12⅞,* and WF/4 fly out of K-6 1955. Weathering around the speed brake on WF/12 has exposed the undercoat. (Eugene S. "Mule" Holmburg via The Tailhook Association Collection)

VMF(N)-513 F3D-2 Skyknights fly in formation over Japan. In the foreground is BuNo 127056, which was part of the third production block, showing overall glossy sea blue with red codes and white aircraft designator and bureau number. The first Skyknights to arrive in Korea during July 1952 were painted flat black but later arrivals retained the overall sea blue coloring. (Tom Doll Rich Dann)

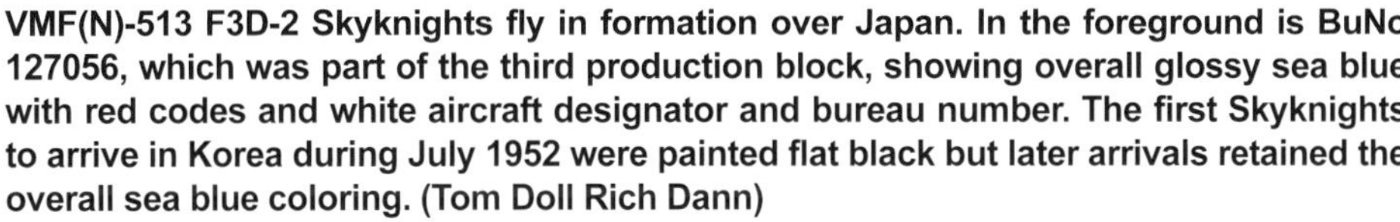

VMF(N)-513 WF/18, BuNo 127027, has reverted to the blue scheme and the tail codes and numbering has reverted from red to white. (SDMA via Mark Aldrich)

VMF(N)-513 remained in East Asia after the Korean War and was based in Japan. WF/2, BuNo 127020, is seen here flying from NAS Atsugi in 1955. (Eugene S. "Mule" Holmburg via Tailhook Association)

A second series F3D-2, BuNo 125836, with in-squadron number WF/23, passes Mt. Fuji, Japan, in 1954 or 1955. VMF(N)-513 operated the F3D-2 and the missile-carrying F3D-2M Skyknight from bases in Japan throughout the 1950s before transitioning to the Douglas F4D Skyray beginning in July 1958. (SDAM via Mark Aldrich)

BuNo 125815 with FALLWEATRAPAC unit code on the aft fuselage under the tail section cruises off Hawaii on 12 November 1952. Its coloring is the standard sea blue with white codes and numbering. (Tailhook Association)

Another composite squadron that operated the Skyknight was VC-33, based out of NAS Atlantic City, New Jersey. The glossy sea blue F3D-2 SS/2 flies over the eastern seaboard on 24 November 1952. (SDMA via Mark Aldrich)

F3D-2s from the "Red Rippers" of VF-11 carry the in-squadron numbers T/101, 102, and 104 in September 1953. The aircraft are painted overall glossy sea blue with red trim bordered in white with white codes and stenciling. (Angelo Romano via Mark Aldrich)

VF-14 ATG/408 is in the air in November 1954. The squadron received the Skyknight in January 1954 and carrier qualified with it in November of the same year. (USN NMNA via Angelo Romano)

VF-14 T/414 has safely returned to NAS Cecil Field after being damaged in a mid-air collision on 18 November 1955. The squadron operated the Skyknight for less than two years before transitioning to the F3H-2 Demon.

The ammunition bin is open on LP/6, unknown bureau number, of Marine Night Fighter Training Squadron 20, VMFT(N)-20, at MCAS Cherry Point, North Carolina, in about 1954. Coloring is overall glossy sea blue with white lettering, numbering, and codes. (USMC)

LP/12, BuNo 125808, at Cherry Point in 1954 or 1955 wears the same coloration as the aircraft seen at left, with red painted caps fitted on the engine intakes and exhausts. (Author's Collection)

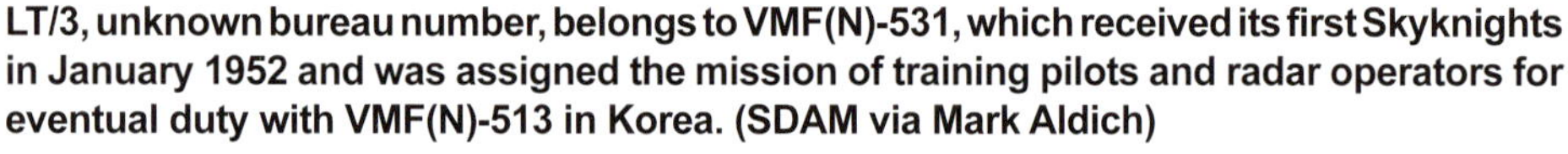

LT/3, unknown bureau number, belongs to VMF(N)-531, which received its first Skyknights in January 1952 and was assigned the mission of training pilots and radar operators for eventual duty with VMF(N)-513 in Korea. (SDAM via Mark Aldich)

Seen here with open speed brake with star and bar painted in the interior in about 1953, LT/14, BuNo 127066, was later converted to an F3D-2Q (EF-10B) operated by VMCJ-1 and 2. (Author's Collection)

F3D-2 LT/13, unknown bureau number, seen here cruising over the eastern seaboard in 1954, belongs to VMF(N)-531 based at MCAS Cherry Point. The squadron was one of four Marine units equipped with the F3D-2 Skyknight. (Major K.D. Edelen USMCR via J.M. Leedle)

"Marines" appears on the lower surface of the wing of LT/19, BuNo 124653. The squadron transitioned to the Douglas F4D Skyray in early 1958. (SDAM via Mark Aldrich)

A flight of VX-4 (Air Development Squadron Four) F3D-2s – consisting of XF/11 (BuNo 125853), #13 (BuNo 125791), #12 (BuNo 125844), and #14 (BuNo 125836) – soar over NAS Point Mugu in 1954 or 1955. (Clay Jansson via Tailhook Association)

VMF(N)-531 F3D-2 in the late 1950s when the tail code was changed from LT to EC, displays black codes with the tail's tip appearing to have been painted red and black. (San Diego Aerospace Museum via Mark Aldrich)

VMF(AW)-542 F3D-2, BuNo 125803, with glossy gray top surfaces and glossy white lower surfaces, rests at Dallas Love Field in the late 1950s. The squadron continued to train night fighter crews with the Skyknight until 1959. (Mark Aldrich)

F3D-2, BuNo 124642, with Navy Parachute Facility at NAS El Centro, California, in July 1960 with glossy gray upper and glossy white lower surfaces. Tail colors are yellow with black lines and white lettering. (Clay Jansson via Tailhook Association)

F-10B, BuNo 124610, with an F-4 Phantom nose and an overall sea blue paint scheme. It was modified by Westinghouse to develop the AN/APQ-72 radar for the Phantom. (Jay Miller Collection via Tommy H. Thomason)

Carrier Operations

Carrier suitability tests with the F3D-2 took place from July to December 1951. Changes to remedy deficiencies found during the initial tests with the XF3D-1 were incorporated in the -2. These modifications improved the aircraft's ability to be launched and recovered. Problems persisted with the Skyknight's suitability to operate successfully aboard a carrier and it was relegated to land-based operations. The aircraft's incompatibility with catapult gear in use at the time made carrier duty problematic for the aircraft. The Skyknight's rated maximum gross weight for a catapult launch – 27,800 pounds – was 10,000 pounds more than the Grumman F9F-5 Panther and pushed the hydraulic catapult to its limit.

The location of the aircraft's tailpipes also caused consternation with carrier personnel since the pipes canted in a downward angle in order to keep engine exhaust away from the aft fuselage. In this configuration, however, the exhaust tended to ignite the older carriers' wooden decks. VC-4 was the only fleet squadron to deploy the F3D-2 from a carrier, with four cruises during 1952 and 1953, including Det-44 that flew from the USS *Champlain* and operated in Korea between April and December 1953. The three other deployments occurred aboard the USS *Roosevelt* (CV-42), which undertook a Mediterranean (Med) Cruise from August to December 1952; the USS *Midway* (CV-41), which conducted another Med Cruise from December 1952 to May 1953; and the USS *Antietam* (CV-36), which cruised off the British coast in June and July 1953.

A landing signal officer guides a Marine Corps F3D-2, possibly LT/19, BuNo 127063, belonging to VMF(N)-531, as it practices a carrier approach at an undisclosed location. (SDAM via Mark Aldrich)

Deck handling crew prepare the second production F3D-1, BuNo 123742, for launch during carrier trials conducted after those performed with the second prototype between October 1949 and February 1950. (Author's Collection)

Number 742 takes off during carrier trials. The markings 742 NATC are marked on the upper wing surface and a large camera reference mark applied next to 742 on the aircraft's fuselage. (SDAM via Mark Aldrich)

F3D-2 BuNo 124596 is prepped to launch. This aircraft had a varied service life beginning with NATC, then on to VX-5, and finally being converted to the EF-10B configuration and serving with VMCJ-3. (SDAM via Mark Aldrich)

F3D-1, possibly BuNo 123743 since it has the code TT-13 below the RO station, lands aboard a carrier during suitability trials conducted sometime after those with the XF3D-1 between October 1949 and February 1950. (SDAM via Mark Aldrich)

F3D-2 BuNo 124598 prepares to be launched from the USS *Midway* (CV-41) while BuNo 124596 prepares to move into position. The Navy conducted a series of accelerated carrier suitability tests with F3D-2, BuNos 124596, 124598, and 124611, between July and December 1951. (NARA)

F3D-2, BuNo 124596, is prepped to launch. This particular aircraft began its career as one of the original carrier suitability aircraft in 1951, then went on to VX-5, and finally, after being converted to the EF-10B configuration, it served with VMCJ-3. (SDAM via Mark Aldrich)

The tailhook of NA/74, BuNo 124545, snares the arresting cable on the USS *Franklin D. Roosevelt* (CV-42) during carrier qualifications in July 1952. A detachment of VC-4 Skyknights served aboard the carrier during a Mediterranean (Med) Cruise. (Emil Buehler Library, NMNA)

NA/74 sit on the deck of USS *Roosevelt*. During the same period squadron detachments operated from 10 carriers. This aircraft was converted to the F3D-2Q/EF-10B configuration and was operated by VMCJ-1 and VMCJ-3. (Emil Buehler Library, NMNA)

NA/71, possibly BuNo 124645, of VC-4 lands aboard the USS *Roosevelt* during the Med Cruise of 1952. VC-4 operated a variety of aircraft, including the F3D-2, F4U-5N, and F6F-5N. (Emil Buehler Library, NMNA)

VF-14 T/402, BuNo 127062, lands on USS *Forrestal* with Deputy Secretary of Defense Reuben B. Robertson Jr. as a passenger. The "A" and "G" have been dropped from the tail code and the nose tip is painted flat gray. (NMNA via Angelo Romano)

VF-14 Douglas F3D Skyknight T/405 (BuNo 125874) lands on USS *Forrestal* (CVA-59) with Assistant Navy Secretary J.H. Smith Jr. as a passenger. VF-14 was one squadron that operated the Skyknight for carrier qualifications only. (NMNA via Angelo Romano)

This unknown Skyknight from VF-14, with gear and tail hook down, prepares to land on an unidentified carrier. This aircraft displays a glossy white nose cone tip while earlier squadron Skyknights wore a solid glossy sea blue. (SDAM via Mark Aldrich)

BuNo 123744, under the control of the Bell Automatic Carrier Landing System (AN/SPN-10), lands on the USS *Antietam* (CVA-36) in August 1957. The "hands off" system was designed to land aircraft in all types of adverse weather conditions. (NARA)

ATG/403 of VF-14 sits aboard the *Intrepid* (CVA-11) during carrier qualifications in November 1954. The squadron did not deploy aboard carriers with the F3D-2; that distinction went to VC-4. (NMNA via Angelo Romano)

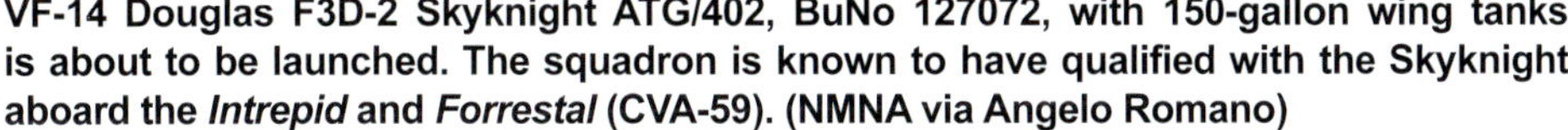

VF-14 Douglas F3D-2 Skyknight ATG/402, BuNo 127072, with 150-gallon wing tanks is about to be launched. The squadron is known to have qualified with the Skyknight aboard the *Intrepid* and *Forrestal* (CVA-59). (NMNA via Angelo Romano)

ATG/404, BuNo 127939, launches from the USS *Intrepid* (CVA-11) on 13 October 1954. It was in October 1954 that the Tophatters carrier qualified on board the *Intrepid*. (Doug Olson via Tailhook Association)

Maintenance personnel inspect the engine of F3D-1, BuNo 123742, in about 1951 at NAS Pax River while the operator of an NC-1 three-wheeled jumpstart jeep waits to provide power for starting the aircraft's engines. The FT designation on the nose stands for Flight Test. This image also shows the three-piece windscreen of the F3D-1 that was replaced by a single-piece on the F3D-2. (NARA)

F3D-2B

The F3D-2B designation was used for F3D aircraft that had special armament capability, beginning with those F3D-1s and F3D-2s that had been reconfigured for the Sparrow I program, (although it appears that this was a paper change only and actual missile-carrying aircraft were not marked in such a manner). The Navy then decided to give the missile-carrying Skyknights their own "M" designation and thereby freed up the "B" designation for special armament again. It appears that 114 F3D-2s were modified as missile or nuclear-carrying Skyknights.

Modifications for the nuclear-carrying F3D included the removal of the two left cannons and the installation of special bombing equipment. The tail warning radar was removed and its control panel was replaced on the radar operator's side of the aircraft with a control panel required for the nuclear-weapon-delivery mission. Reinforced wing pylons allowed the aircraft to carry either one MK-7 or one MK-12 nuclear bomb. The MK-7 was the first nuclear weapon that could be carried by Air Force and Navy fighters and had a variable yield of 8, 19, 22, 31, and 61 kilotons. The MK-12 had a 12-14 kiloton yield. The weapon was mounted on the right pylon with an associated 300-gallon or 150-gallon fuel tank on the left pylon (a 300-gallon tank/MK-7 and 150-gallon tank/MK-12 configuration).

It appears the planes were delivered to the Navy between January and May 1953 with Air Test and Evaluation Squadrons Five (VX-5) operating approximately eight of this variant from Point Mugu and China Lake, California, between 1953 and 1957. BuNo 127044, as the prototype for a nuclear bomb-carrying variant of the F3D-2, is the only known Skyknight to actually have the -B designation applied to it.

Parked at NAS Oakland on 18 October 1953, BuNo 127044 of Navy squadron VX-5 was one of only about eight Skyknights to carry the F3D-2B designation. It was modified to carry nuclear weapons. (WT Larkins and Clay Jansson via Tailhook Association)

F3D-2M

In 1962, Douglas Aircraft delivered 16 F3D-2M planes designated as MF-2B. The bureau numbers of these aircraft were 125822, 125837, 125847, 125857, 125867, 125872, 125877, 125882, 127023, 127028, 127033, 127038, 127043, 127048, 127053, and 127058. The conversion primarily consisted of fitting underneath the outboard and inboard wing four hard points for launching Sparrow missiles, similar to the F3D-1M. The Dash-2M, however, had a larger nose cone to house the Sperry AN/APQ-36 radar and the four nose-mounted 20mm cannons were removed. Only about half of the aircraft actually received the APQ-36 system, however. VX-4, VMF(N)-513, and -542 operated the missile-carrying Skyknight until late in the 1950s, when the 513 and 542 transitioned to the Douglas F4D Skyray. Those missile-carrying Skyknights left in the Navy inventory by 1962 were redesignated as the MF-10B.

Douglas, building on the concept of the F3D-2M, was awarded a contract by the U.S. Navy in December 1958 to develop the F6D-1 Missileer, designed as a subsonic missile platform to carry as many as six Bendix-Grumman AAM-N-10 Eagle missiles and destroy enemy bombers.

The aircraft was to be equipped with the Westinghouse AN/APQ-81 radar, capable of detecting targets at 120 nautical miles, tracking up to eight targets from 80 nautical miles, and launching its supersonic missiles with a range of 110 nautical miles. This program, however, was cancelled before a prototype was constructed. Another proposal was for the construction of an F3D-3, a swept wing version of the aircraft that would be capable of carrying a variety of external stores. This program, however, was also canceled.

BuNo 127038 was the first conversion model for the F3D-2M and featured four wing mounts for missiles and had an extended nose to house the APS-36 radar. The aircraft is overall sea blue with white codes and markings. (SDAM via Mark Aldrich)

Commander Ken Thayer of VX-4 is at the controls of F3D-2M XF-7, unknown bureau number, during Project Steam evaluation tests aboard the U.S.S *Hancock* (CVA-19) on 30 June 1954. Air Development Squadron Four (VX-4) based at Point Mugu, California, evaluated air-launched missile systems for the Navy. (Tommy H. Thomason)

The tailhook of a Sparrow I armed F3D-2M, BuNo 127043, snags the wire aboard the USS *Hancock* in June 1954. F3D-2M aircraft used for missile tests were equipped with cameras mounted in the ammunition storage bins. (Tommy H. Thomason)

An F3D-2M, BuNo 125487, WH/16 of VMF(AW)-542 in 1957 at NAS Dallas, Texas. The squadron became the first Marine missile fighter squadron in 1954 after receiving a number of F3D-2M aircraft from VX-4. (Mark Aldrich)

Former Naval Missile Test Center YF3D-2M, BuNo 127028, rests in storage at Davis Monthan AFB (MASDC) in the early 1960s with a reinforcement brace attached to the wing mount. Coloring includes black codes, red engine stripes, blue main wheels, flat anti-glare panel, and a flat black nose tip. (Clay Jansson via Tailhook Association)

The speed brake is deployed on WH/15, BuNo 125872. This aircraft, which features the larger nose cone of the F3D-2M, has overall period colors with a faded flat black nose, black codes, red engine stripes, and aluminum leading edges. (Tom Doll via Rich Dann)

F3D-2T / F3D-2T2

Ten F3D-2s were modified as F3D-2T night fighter trainers (BuNos 124595, 124605, 124607, 124622, 124627, 124635, 124638, 124629, 124658, and 127022) while another 55 were designated as the F3D-2T2, which was used to train radar operators for the McDonnell Douglas F-4 Phantom. The -2T used the Westinghouse AP-50 radar also found in the Douglas F4D Skyray while the -2T2 utilized the AN/APG-51B radar system that was standard on the F3H-2N Demon. The -2Ts were subsequently modified to the -2T2 configuration with the last change to the -2T2 variant consisting of changing the radar system from the APG-51B to the APG-51C.

The F3D could handle a variety of changes to its electronic systems (for example, changing from the AN/APQ-36 to the APG-51) as the fuselage's size and sturdiness allowed it to accommodate an enormous amount of electronics. The space was needed in that era of vacuum tubes that resulted in large, bulky systems weighing up to several hundred pounds.

Navy and Marine squadrons that operated the F3D-2T and/or the F3D-2T2 included China Lake, the Fleet All-Weather Training Unit Pacific (FAWTUPAC), the Heavy Attack Training Unit Pacific (HATUPAC), the Navy Air Development Unit (NADU), VFAW-3, the Fleet All-Weather Training Unit Atlantic (FAWTULANT), VF-101, VF-121, VMFT(N)-20, VMFT(AW)-20, VT-86, and VX-4. In 1962, the designation for the F3D-2T2 was changed to the TF-10B.

Chief of Naval Operations Adm. Arleigh A. Burke and pilot Cdr. Selden May, CO of Navy Guided Missile Unit 61 (GMU-61), conduct a preflight walkaround of F3D-2T, BuNo 124616, at China Lake on 14 April 1959. (U.S. Navy via Gary Verver)

BuNo 124595 has been converted to an F3D-2T and used to test missile and radar systems. This image shows the aircraft with the AGM-45 Cobra, the prototype for the AGM-45 Shrike missile, at China Lake on 24 May 1960. (U.S. Navy via Gary Verver)

An F3D-2T2 operated by VF-101 Det A, AD/180 in August 1958 is an all glossy sea blue with FAWTULANT yellow markings. As a training squadron, VF-101 was based at NAS Oceana, Virginia. (Clay Jansson via Tailhook Association)

XF/3, BuNo 124639, of VX-4 is seen at NAS North Island on 12 September 1959. Its coloring is gray on upper surfaces with white on forward lower surfaces, day-glo orange on the nose and aft portion of wings, fuselage, and tail. (Mike Napolitano Collection via Coronado Historical Association and Mark Aldrich)

VF-101 operated F3D-2T2s for training F3H Demon and later F4B pilots. AD/176, BuNo 124607, is shown here at NAS Oceana, Virginia, in about 1960. The aircraft coloration is standard for training aircraft of the period with glossy white and day-glo orange. (Clay Jansson via Tailhook Association)

A lightning bolt and green turtle have been applied to the fuselage of NJ/197, BuNo 124597, at NAS Miramar in about 1960. VF-121 was the West Coast sister squadron of VF-101. (Clay Jansson via Tailhook Association)

In May 1961, China Lake F-10B BuNo 125807 is wearing the distinctive orange and white coloration applied to training aircraft. The aircraft previously served with VC-4, VF-11, VF-14, and VF-101. (Clay Jansson via Tailhook Association)

VF-121 F3D-2T2 NJ/195 and NJ/198 BuNo 124638 at NAS Marimar in 1960 wear the paint scheme adopted by the Navy in 1959 for jet training aircraft. Each displays different variations of Semi-Gloss Fluorescent Orange and Glossy Insignia White. (Tailhook Association via Rich Dann)

This front view of NJ/197, BuNo 124597, at Marimar NAS in June 1960 shows the 20mm cannon ports without the in-squadron number as displayed on NJ/199 in the previous image. (Clay Jannson via Tailhook Association)

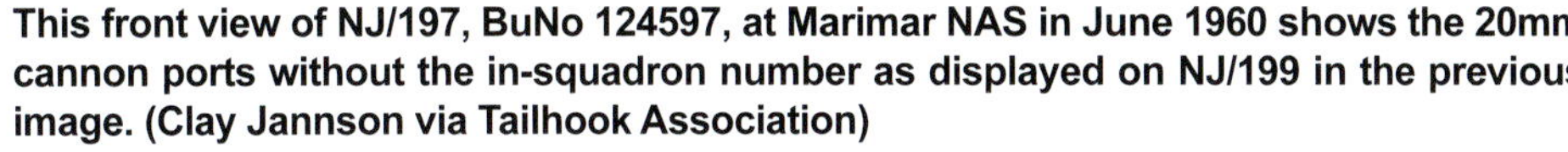

FAWTUPAC was redesignated as VF(AW)-3 in May 1958. The new designation is shown here on F3D-2T2, BuNo 125824, with #143 applied to both sides of the fuselage, at NAS North Island in 1961. (Clay Jansson via Rich Dann)

F3D-2T2 NJ/198, this time with 124617, is seen at NAS Miramar on 2 June 1960. The squadron was one of the Navy's Replacement Air Group (RAG) training squadrons and Skyknights were used to train F3H pilots and F4H Phantom II pilots and Radar Intercept Officers (RIOs). (Clay Jannson via Tailhook Association)

The in-squadron number is barely visible on the starboard wing of VF-121 F3D-2T2 NJ/199, BuNo 127081, at Miramar in July 1960. (Clay Jansson via Tailhook Association)

PA/17 FAWTUPAC, BuNo 125870, wears a gray-and-white scheme with flat black leading edges, nose tip, anti-glare panel, and red intake lips on 29 September 1955. The squadron served as an all-weather training squadron and flew the Skyknight from 1952 to 1963. (SDAM via Mark Aldrich)

Ordnancemen load 20mm cannons on FAWTUPAC F3D-2T2 at NAS North Island 1958. (Mark Nankivil via Rich Dann)

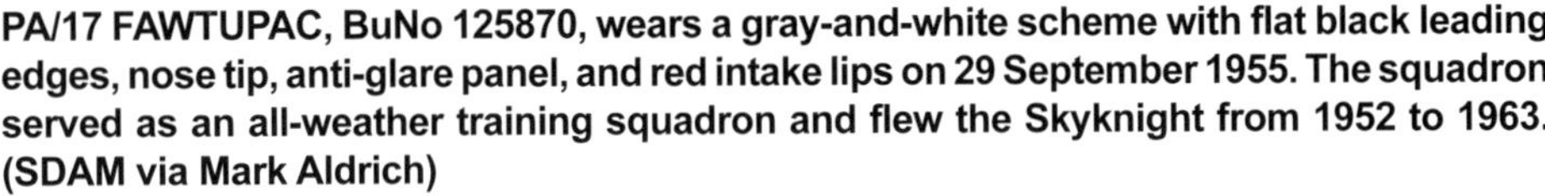

VF(AW)-3 PA/7, BuNo 124617, at Paine AFB, Washington, during May 1958 displays typical coloring for the era but with a faded dirty brown nose tip and noticeable residue from the cannons. (Author's Collection)

A FAWTUAC pilot and RO rush to an F3D-2T2 in a staged alert at NAS North island near San Diego, California, in 1958 with PA/16, BuNo 127019, in the background. (Mark Nankivil via Rich Dann)

FAWTUPAC Pilot and RO climb onto PA/11 during a staged alert at NAS North Island in 1958. The aircraft was assigned to the 27th North American Air Defense Command. (Mark Nankivil collection via Rich Dann)

PA/14, BuNo 124611, prepares to depart from North Island in about 1958. This aircraft was used in carrier trials in 1952. Behind PA/14 are other Skyknights that still retain the blue coloring. (SDAM via Mark Aldrich)

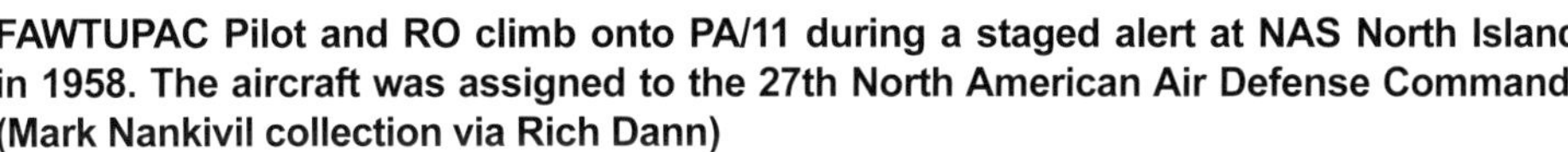
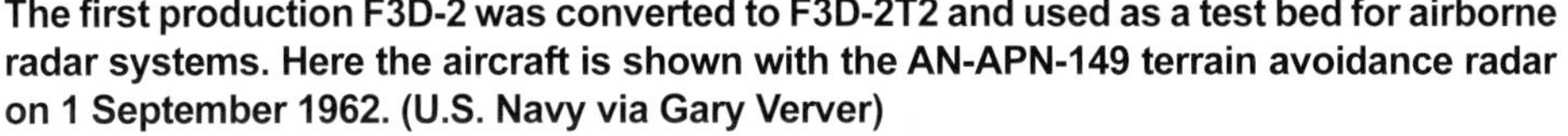

The first production F3D-2 was converted to F3D-2T2 and used as a test bed for airborne radar systems. Here the aircraft is shown with the AN-APN-149 terrain avoidance radar on 1 September 1962. (U.S. Navy via Gary Verver)

The stains visible below the cannon port on FAWTUPAC BuNo 124613 are the result of firing the weapons. There are also exhaust stains on the bottom rear fuselage. (SDAM via Mark Aldrich)

Armed with a Shrike missile, TF-10B BuNo 124630 waits on the tarmac at China Lake on 7 February 1964. The aircraft's coloring is glossy white on the lower fuselage with day-glo orange tail, banded white and orange wings, and an orange band around nose. (U.S. Navy via Gary Verver)

BuNo 127074, seen here during the mid-1960s, was later used to test the North American Aviation XR-45 automatic terrain-following and air-to-ground radar system. (SDAM via Mark Aldrich)

The unusual nose of TF-10B BuNo 127074, pictured here at China Lake on 21 March 1963, houses the AN/APQ-89 terrain-following radar. The system was also tested in the North American T-2C Buckeye. (U.S. Navy via Gary Verver)

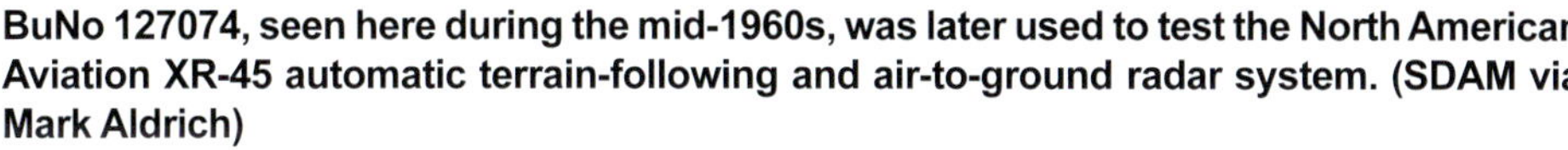

To test and evaluate its Surface-to-Air (SAM) defensive and offensive systems, China Lake modified BuNo 124630 with an A-4 Skyhawk nose, including a nonfunctional inflight refueling probe. (U.S. Navy via Gary Verver)

TF-10B BuNo 124630 with A4 Skyhawk nose is parked at China Lake on 16 March 1967. At least four Skyknights were fitted with modified noses to test new radar systems. (Clay Jansson via Rich Dann)

TF-10B BuNo 125879, seen here at NAS Glynco, Georgia, on 21 June 1963, was used for navigational training. Prior to its transfer to Navy Training Squadron 86 (VT-86), the aircraft served with VF-101. (Robert Dorr)

F3D-2Q

The Skyknight's primary mission and designation as the F3D-2 night fighter changed during the late 1950s to that of the F3D-2Q, the Marines' first jet electronic warfare (EW) aircraft with electronic countermeasures (ECM) and electronic intelligence (ELINT) capabilities with the purpose of intercepting and jamming radar transmissions. The modification of the F3D-2 to the E-10B allowed the Skyknight to become the only jet aircraft to serve in both the Korean and Vietnam Wars. Marine Composite Reconnaissance Squadron Three (VMCJ-3) initiated the conversion program as airframe change (AFC-173) at MCAS El Toro, California, in 1955, with F3D-2 BuNos 124620 and 125786 designated as F3D-2Qs in February 1956 (designated as the EF-10B in 1962).

Major ECM and ELINT electronics gear consisted of the following: AN/APR-9/13 tuners, AN/APA-69 Direction Finding Radar Set used in conjunction with the AN/ALR-8 receiving system with panoramic indicator, AN/ALT-2 Airborne Noise Spot Jamming Transmitter, and AN/APR-13 Panoramic Radar Intercept Receiver. In a formal modification program, the Navy Rework Facility at North Island reconfigured 35 aircraft as the F3D-2Q. VMCJ-3 took delivery of its first production aircraft BuNo 124602 in December 1956 with the squadron completing its transition from the Douglas AD-4N/5N Skyraider to the F3D-2Q in 1957. Three Marine squadrons, VMCJ-1, VMCJ-2, and VMCJ-3, operated the F3D-2Q between 1956 and 1969. VMCJ-3 with nine F3D-2Qs deployed to MCAS Iwakuni, Japan, in August 1958, and ran EW missions called "Sharkfin" around the periphery of China, North Korea, and the Soviet Union to investigate the radar abilities of U.S. Cold War adversaries. The mission continued when the Golden Hawks of VMCJ-1 took custody of VMCJ-3's Skyknights and replaced that unit in November 1959. On the east coast, VMCJ-2, nicknamed the Playboys, based at MCAS Cherry Point, North Carolina, replaced its AD-5Ns with the Skyknight in 1958.

The Cuban Revolution and Fidel Castro's growing relationship with the Soviet Union greatly concerned the U.S. VMCJ-2 began flying electronic reconnaissance or ELINT missions around Cuba beginning in September 1960, primarily from Key West, Guantánamo Bay, and Puerto Rico. During the next two years the squadron monitored the build-up of Soviet radars in Cuba and its Electronic Countermeasure Officers (ECMO) were the first to intercept TOKEN ground control intercept, Fire Can and Whiff anti-aircraft artillery (AAA) fire control radar. In August 1962 two F3D-2Qs were the first to report intercepting the Fan Song target tracking radar employed with the Soviet SA-2 surface-to-air missile (SAM). VMCJ-2 Skyknights were also tagged to be the main assets to perform ECM against Soviet/Cuban air defenses in case airstrikes were ordered to take out missile sites prior to invasion. After the U.S. negotiated the withdrawal of Soviet nuclear missiles from Cuba, VMCJ continued to fly periodic electronic reconnaissance missions of Cuba. The squadron received the Navy Unit Commendation for its efforts from 1 September 1960 to 1 December 1962.

CY/15, BuNo 124620, with VMCJ-2 codes, is painted an overall glossy white with black codes and antiglare panel. The rudder, wing tips, nose, and the nose and tail of the drop tank are painted day-glo orange. (SDAM via Mark Aldrich)

Seen here in 1959 or 1960, VMCJ-2 CY-20, BuNo 125809, was one of 35 Skyknights converted to the F3D-2Q configuration beginning in 1955. The designation for the EW-configured Skyknight changed to EF-10B in 1962. (Arthur O'Keefe Collection via Tailhook Association)

In the front of this flight line of VMCJ-2 F3D-2Q Skyknights is CY/16 BuNo 127050, which went on to operate with VMCJ-1 in Vietnam. After suffering extensive AAA battle damage in Indochina, the aircraft was assigned as a parts plane in 1965. (SDAM via Mark Aldrich)

Another view of VMCJ-2 Skyknights with the bureau numbers of the first two planes, BuNos 124618 and 125833, visible in the foreground along with the last, BuNo 127072. (Author's Collection)

EF-10Bs were equipped with external ECM pods and chaff dispensers. A close-up view of this VMCJ-2 reveals an opening at the bottom of the pod that marks it as a chaff dispenser.

A veteran of VMF(N)-513 and the Korean War, F3D-2Q BuNo 124618, seen here as VMCJ-2 CY/18 during the late 1950s, later went on to Vietnam service with VMCJ-1 and was finally retired as a VMCJ-3 EF-10B. (Emil Buehler Library, NMNA)

Heavy residue from the aircraft's engine exhausts streaks the glossy white finish on the underside of BuNo 127047 during the early 1960s. After operating with VMCJ-1 and 2 the aircraft ended up at AMARC where it was scrapped. (Joseph H. Schvimmer)

After participating in the Cuban Missile Crisis, CY/16 went to VMCJ-1 for service in Vietnam. It was later one of the last two EF-10Bs to leave Vietnam on 25 October 1969. (Joseph H. Schvimmer)

VMCJ-2 F3D-2Q CY/16, BuNo 127047, displays the squadron's playboy bunny logo at NAS Pax River in December 1965. The squadron conducted ELINT missions, monitoring Cuban radar and radio signals from 1960 to 1962. (Dick Hill via Tailhook Association)

Another formation of F3D-2Qs from VMCJ-3 with BuNo 124596 in the foreground, followed by BuNos 125806, 125850, and 127060 is seen on 12 May 1958. Three of the aircraft – BuNos 125806, 125850, and 127060 – went on to see service with VMCJ-1 in Vietnam, with 125806 being lost in action in 1965. (SDAM via Mark Aldrich)

Seen here possibly in the early 1960s, TN/6, BuNo 124596, with VMCJ-3 was the second production F3D-2 that took part in the original carrier suitability tests during 1951. After operating for a few months with VMCJ-3 in 1958, VMCJ-1 took control of the aircraft and kept it in its inventory until the fall of 1960, when it was transferred back to VMCJ-3. (Author's Collection)

VMCJ-3 BuNos 125831, 125850, 127060, and an unknown aircraft fly by Mt. Fuji, Japan. The squadron was based at MCAS Iwakuni, Japan, during 1958 and 1959. TN-15 was lost with its crew in Vietnam on 16 January 1968. (USMC)

EF-10B VMCJ-3 BuNo 124663 is staged for an airshow at MCAS El Toro, California, during the early 1960s. (Author's Collection)

The third F3D-2Q prototype modified at North Island, EF-10B BuNo 124602, seen here at El Toro during the early 1960s, joined VMCJ-3 in November 1956. (Author's Collection)

BuNo 125786 from VMCJ-3 still bears the F3D-2 designation in this image from NAS North Island, possibly shot during the time the aircraft was being reconfigured as the second F3D-2Q prototype in late 1955. Behind it on the left is a P4Y-2K Privateer target drone. Three F3D2s – BuNos 124596, 124620, and 124602 – underwent reconfiguring by VMC-3, later VMCJ-3, for EW purposes to replace the squadron's Douglas AD-5Ns. The first two prototypes were designated F3D-2Q in 1956 and the third not long after with the formal modification program known as Airframe Change 173. VMCJ-1 operated this aircraft from Đà Nẵng, South Vietnam. It was lost along with its crew, Capt. Joseph P. Murphy and 2Lt. Walter L. Albright, on 24 March 1967. (AAHS)

EF-10B in Vietnam

In East Asia, the U.S. commitment to Vietnam intensified on 2 March 1965 when the Air Force launched Operation Rolling Thunder, a sustained bombing campaign against targets in North Vietnam, in an effort to end the North's support of the Viet Cong in the South. A week later, on 9 March, the Ninth Marine Expeditionary Brigade (MEB) landed in Vietnam to protect the airfield at Da Nang. The presence of Fire Can sites in North Vietnam meant that EW aircraft were needed to identify and jam enemy radar during airstrikes. That mission went to the Air Force's EB-66C Destroyer and the Marine's EF-10B Skyknight. On 17 April 1965, VMCJ-1's Lt. Colonel Otis Wes Corman led a detachment of six EF-10Bs from their base at Iwakuni, Japan, to Da Nang and joined a Marine F-4B squadron VMFA-531. Attached administratively to MAG-16 they were under the operational control of the Air Force's 2nd Air Division.

The detachment's Skyknights had two spot jamming devices installed in the nose and the aircraft could carry external wing-mounted jamming pods containing four noise and deception jammers. The latter were designed to deceive enemy radar by broadcasting a false return and were also equipped with a chaff dispenser. However, since an EF-10B could only jam enemy radar located in front of the aircraft, at least two Skyknights were needed to support a strike mission. The Skyknights, operating ahead of the attacking force, would set up a racetrack pattern where one of the two aircraft was always heading towards the target, jamming enemy radar.

The Skyknight lacked aerial refueling capability. To extend its range, the aircraft carried two 300-gallon auxiliary fuel tanks; one if a wing-mounted ALQ-31 Pod, housing ECM jammers, was employed. Despite the extra fuel, Marine pilots often shut down one of the engines to conserve fuel while descending from their operational altitude of 30,000 to 35,000 feet on their return to Da Nang. The added weight and drag caused by the fuel tank significantly reduced the rate of climb of a fully loaded EF-10B, so the aircraft took off towards the sea to avoid small arms fire from Viet Cong guerrillas operating near the airfield. VMCJ-1 first supported the 2nd Air Division and Task Force 77 with a typical support mission involving at least two aircraft flying a circular orbit, with the target in the center. At an altitude of 20,000-26,000 feet, the aircraft dropped chaff and transmitted jamming signals against Fire Can gun control, early warning, and GCI radar while strike aircraft conducted the bombing mission. Additionally, EF-10Bs attempted to locate and jam Fan Song sites while operating with bombers during night interdiction missions.

The squadron's first combat mission to jam North Vietnamese Army (NVA) radar sites was conducted on 29 April 1965 in support of an Air Force strike. During May and June, the EF-10B operated at 300 percent of normal utilization but, by July, due to a lack of aircraft and spare parts, each Skyknight was limited to a utilization rate of 200 percent or a monthly operation of 60 hours per plane. Maintaining this ability required the 1st MAW to assign a liaison officer to Military Assistance Command Vietnam's (MACV) electronic warfare coordinating authority to ensure that VMCJ-1 was only tasked to support Air Force and Navy operations in only high-threat areas, such as inside the SA-2 missile envelope complex around Hanoi. The first SAM site was detected on 5 April, another

Lance Cpl. Robert C. Anderson, a mechanic with VMCJ-1, poses in one of the squadron's EF-10Bs in December 1965. The red missile symbols, and sometimes lightning bolts, indicate the number jamming missions undertaken by this plane, identified only as RM/7. (Author's Collection)

VMCJ-1 RM/5, BuNo 125849, was one of six EF-10B Skyknights that participated in the first air strike against SAM missile sites over North Vietnam under the code name Spring High on 27 July 1965. (Robert Dorr)

in May, and corresponding Fan Song radar was reported by a USAF EB-66C on 23 July. The day after the radar's detection, one of four F-4C Phantoms, flying MiG Combat Air Patrol (MIGCAP) for Republic F-105D Thunderchief fighter-bombers (Thuds) 40 miles southwest of Hanoi near the Black River, was shot down by an SA-2 and the other three Phantoms were damaged by missile hits.

In response to this new threat, the Air Force called for a massive strike against the missile sites on 27 July by 48 Thuds backed by 12 F4-C Phantoms and Lockheed 104-C Starfighters flying MiGCAP. Six VMCJ-1's EF-10Bs were called upon to provide EW support for the strike force, which was code-named Spring High. Five Whales departed together, followed 15 minutes later by another EF-10B, without fighter support. They were briefed to arrive over Haiphong Harbor, turn west 75 miles to their initial point 35 miles SSE of Hanoi, and then set up the standard racetrack pattern over the SAM sites at 20,000 feet. Passing over Thanh Hoa one of the EF-10Bs picked up 15 fire control radars tracking the EF-10Bs and the aircraft began jamming. The Thuds arrived and commenced their strike against the missile sites as the four EW aircraft jammed fire control, GCI, and enemy communications, while trying to evade heavy AAA flak. Although the Whales were effective in jamming the SAMs, none of which was launched during the engagement, the strike was one of the blackest days for the USAF. Six F-105s operating at lower altitudes, were lost to ground fire. Another Thud suffered severe damage after encountering a barrage of SAMs and heavy AAA later that day during a follow-up strike, conducted without EW support from VMCJ-1, against remaining targets in the area. Intelligence later determined that most of the missile batteries were dummy sites and the NVA had actually moved the SA-2s.

The EF-10s were in high demand as they, along with eight EB-66C Destroyers, were the only EW aircraft available during 1965. The "Whales" alone accounted for 791 support missions over North Vietnam and Laos, in the course of which VMCJ-1 lost one F-10B and crew. Four days after the 27 July mission, RM-8 BuNo 125806 crashed into the sea shortly after takeoff from Da Nang, killing 1st Lt. Milton K. McNulty and CWO-2 Vernard J. Small. Four more Skyknights and crews would perish through accidents or unknown causes during the next two years of operations. VMCJ-1's mixed bag of Chance-Vought RF-8A, RF-4B, EA-6A, and EF-10B aircraft conducted over 3,700 photographic reconnaissance, radar and communication jamming sorties over Vietnam during 1966, with the squadron's Skyknights and Intruders conducting more than 60 percent of all ECM and ELINT missions for Rolling Thunder. Brigadier General Hugh M. Elwood, assistant MAW-1 commander, commented on the importance of the squadron's EW capability by stating, "It was a fact that Seventh Fleet did not launch against Hanoi until a VMCJ ECM plane from Da Nang was on station."

EF-10B crews rarely ventured away from their purpose but on a couple of occasions

EF-10B BuNo 125869 appears on display at an air show at NAS Dallas, Texas, in 1966. The aircraft lacks a tail code but the bureau number indicates that it belonged to VMCJ-1 and saw service in Vietnam. (Author's Collection)

they were called upon to provide close-air support and photo recon and each time the crews were reprimanded for endangering the precious few EF-10Bs at the Navy's disposal. On 1 March 1966, 1st Lt. Ken Crouch and Capt. Jim Gazzale provided close-air support for American ground forces after receiving a request from a USAF Forward Air Controller (FAC). Fire from the aircraft's 20mm cannon on a couple strafing runs was credited with two Viet Cong KIA.

The only known loss of an EF-10B to enemy action occurred on 18 March 1966 when one of two EF-10Bs, escorted by Marine F-4B Phantoms, was shot down while supporting four F-105s hitting targets in and around the North Vietnamese city of Thanh Hoa, located inside a known SAM ring. The two Skyknights with the call signs Riverboat One and Riverboat Two departed Da Nang at 0730 with Capt. Bill Bergmann with 1st Lt. Wayne "Flash" Whitten aboard Riverboat One and 1st Lt. Everett "Mac" McPherson and 1st Lt. Brent Davis in Riverboat Two. Whitten picked up a Fan Song SAM target tracking radar as the flight crossed into North Vietnam and believed it came from the Vinh area which was near their planned flight track north. Whitten broadcast a warning to the rest of the flight and began jamming a Fire Can AAA radar threatening the Thuds.

The EF-10B was able to provide a measure of protection to other aircraft inside a SAM envelope, however, its own jamming strobes made it vulnerable to tracking by a Fan Song and, since their missions were usually flown straight and level above 20,000 feet, it was highly susceptible to an SA-2 missile. Perhaps 1st Lt. Davis aboard McPherson's aircraft was intent on jamming the Fire Can in the target area. In any case, in front of Bergmann, approximately 10 miles west of Thanh Hoa City and at an altitude of 26,000 feet, Riverboat Two disappeared in a ball of fire as a SAM slammed into the aircraft. Neither Riverboat One nor the escorting Phantoms saw any chutes deploy. The Joint MIA/POW Accounting Command (JPAC) recovered the remains of Lt. Davis in 1997 but those of McPherson remain missing.

VMCJ-1 continued to operate both the EF-10B and EA-6A Intruder in support of Rolling Thunder through 1967, 1968, and most of 1969, during which time, three more aircraft and their crews were lost. Capt. Joseph P. Murphy and Walter L. Albright were killed when RM-2 (BuNo 125786), which was the second EF-10B prototype modified in February 1956, crashed during a maintenance flight near Da Nang on 24 March 1967. The squadron suffered two more losses in 1968. On 16 January that year, RM-4 (BuNo 125831) crashed at sea for unknown reasons, killing Capt. William D. Moreland and 1st Lt. Paul S. Gee. Then on 19 July, Capt. Lionel Parra and 1st Lt. Ariel L. Cross failed to return from a night mission along the Demilitarized Zone.

The last EF-10B modification program, airframe change 199 (AFC-199), occurred at the Naval Rework Facility, North Island, when EF-10B BuNo 124620 underwent an upgrade of its ECM and Avionics with the installation of the APR-27 and APR-33 missile/fire control warning receivers and updated communications equipment in August 1967. Members of VMCJ-3 tested the new equipment at the Naval Missile Test Center, Point Mugu. Reconfigured were the "Super Whale," nickname of BuNo 124620, and eight other EF-10Bs: BuNos 124618, 124645, 125810, 125818, 125846, 127034, 127047, and 127060. All but BuNo 124618 had Vietnam service. In February 1968, the

Pilots and Radar Operators of VMCJ-1 gather in front of the second F3D-2Q prototype RM/2 BuNo 125786. This plane and crew were lost in Vietnam on 24 March 1967. (Author's Collection)

Seen here at Đà Nẵng in 1966, EF-10B RN/3, BuNo 127051, was damaged when a tire exploded aboard her in flight in August 1966. Subsequently the aircraft served as a source for spare parts. (Robert Dorr)

First Lieutenant Wayne "Flash" Whitten poses on the former VMCJ-3 BuNo 125831 now bearing RM/4 at Đà Nẵng in 1966. This aircraft crashed off the coast of Vietnam due to unknown causes with the loss of the crew on 16 January 1968. (Robert Dorr)

Formerly belonging to VMCJ-2, BuNo 125809, RM/8 with three EW mission markings, is seen here landing at Đà Nẵng in February or March 1967. (Rich Dann)

last full year of EF-10B operations in Vietnam, three "Super Whales," BuNos 124620, 125810, and 125846, arrived at Da Nang.

By 1969, the Skyknight had become an antiquated airframe with few replacement aircraft or spare parts to sustain operations. It became a second-line asset with the arrival in Da Nang of additional E6-A Intruders with their more advanced EW capabilities. The last Skyknight EW support mission in Vietnam took place on 2 October, with Capt. J.J. Morrissey and his ECMO 1st Lt. Fiegler, flying BuNo 124645. The last EF-10B left Vietnam for the United States on 25 October 1969. The Skyknight's active service with the Marines concluded in May 1970 when Colonel O.R. Davis, commanding officer of MAG-33, took off from El Toro MCAS and flew the former VMCJ-3 EF-10B (BuNo 124618) to the Marine Corps Museum at Quantico, Virginia. Colonel Davis was the same pilot who made the first night time MiG-15 kill over Korea on 8 November 1952 while flying an F3D-2 with VMF(N)-513.

After the last EF-10B left Vietnam in the fall of 1969, the life of a few Skyknight variants extended into the late 1980s to 30 June 1987 with the Raytheon Corporation utilizing three flyable Skyknights, BuNos 124598, 124630, and 125807 to test Army missile defense systems from Holloman Air Force Base, New Mexico and China Lake. Five additional aircraft held in storage at Davis Monthan AFB, Arizona, consisting of F-10B BuNo 124610 and EF-10Bs BuNos 124620, 124633, 125850, 127047 along with former China Lake BuNo 127074 that was flown to Hanscon AFB, Massachusetts, were held as a source for spare parts. The last two flyable were returned to the Navy in exchange for two Grumman A-7 Corsair IIs.

RM/5, BuNo 125849, at Đà Nẵng in February or March 1967 sports 30 red EW markings. Aft of the cockpit is a yellow warning stripe with black lettering. (Tom Hansen via Tailhook Association)

VMCJ-1 RM/3 BuNo 127051, seen at Đà Nẵng in about the summer of 1966, was flown by Captain Bill Bergmann and 1st Lt. Wayne "Flash" Whitten on the mission where Lts. Davis and McPherson were lost. (MSgt W.F. Gemeinhart, USMC via Tailhook Association)

RM/9, BuNo 124632, seen at Đà Nẵng during February or March 1967, has two EW mission marks and displays a slight variation of the in-squadron numbering system with small #9s on the tail. (Tom Hansen via Tailhook Association)

The first F3D-2Q prototype BuNo 124620, seen here as RM/2 at MCAS El Toro, California, was upgraded as a Super Whale EF-10B. (Tailhook Association via Rich Dann)

TN/5 VMCJ-3 EF-10B BuNo 125846 at MCAS El Toro during the mid-1960s was later reconfigured as the second super whale and was delivered to VMCJ-1 at Đà Nẵng, South Vietnam, on 26 February 1968. (Mark Aldrich)

The Raytheon Corporation operated BuNo 124630 during the 1970s and mid-1980s before the Flying Leathernecks Historical Foundation acquired it and painted the aircraft in the colors of VMF(N)-513. (Author's Collection)

Three Skyknights were delivered to the Raytheon Corporation for testing of radar systems during the late 1970s. This F-10B, BuNo 124598, with Army markings, is painted an overall glossy sea blue. (AAHS)

The Raytheon Corporation operated BuNo 124630 during the 1970s and mid-1980s before the Flying Leathernecks Historical Foundation acquired it and painted the aircraft in the colors of VMF(N)-513. (John D. Voss)

Douglas F-10B BuNo 124610, with F-4 nose at Davis Monthan AFB in the early 1960s, served Raytheon as a parts plane through the late 1980s. (Clay Jansson via Rich Dann)

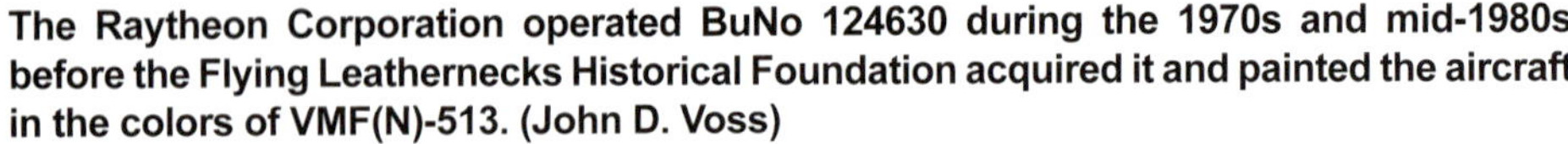

EF-10B TN/4, BuNo 124618, seen at Quantico, Virginia, in Spring 1976, was an original VMF(N)-513 F3D-2 before being modified to the EF-10B configuration. (Robert Dorr)

TN/4 at Quantico originally was operated by VMCJ-2 during the Cuba crisis before ending its service life with VMCJ-3. It is now located at the National Museum of the Marine Corps. (Robert Dorr)